BEYOND BOUNDARIES: THRIVING IN LIFE'S GREY ZONE

Compiled by: Dr. Constance Leyland

Level Up Academy by Doc Leyland

LEVEL ᴜᑭ
Higher Education Edition

First Edition

ISBN: 979-8-218-40139-9

Anthology copyright notice:

Contributor Copyrights:

Cover design by: Front cover by
Dr. Constance Leyland;
the back of the book was designed by
Cyndal Dunn (picture only)

Dedication

To the fearless explorers of life's grey zones, this book, *Beyond Boundaries: Thriving in Life's Grey Zone,* is dedicated to you. Through the diverse perspectives of 27 unique authors, we journey into the complexities of human experience, exploring the nuanced spaces where life doesn't offer clear black-and-white answers. Each author, with their distinct voice and insights, contributes to a collage of understanding that challenges, inspires, and encourages us to embrace the uncertainty of the grey zones.

Together, they illuminate the paths of resilience, growth, and transformation that lie hidden in the shadows of ambiguity. May their collective wisdom guide you to navigate life's intricacies with grace, courage, and an open heart, inspiring you to find your own way beyond boundaries.

Table of Contents

Living in the gray zone: I am worthy of love even as broken as I am

By: Crystal Behe

Do you feel like you are not good enough to be loved? Were you broken by a previous spouse or close friend or in your current relationship? Did they tell you that no one will want you after them? Well, I am proof that you are worthy of finding love again and having a healthy, thriving relationship.

I want you to imagine a woman in her late thirties who is so broken and beaten down that she is ready to give up. The relationship she had been in for the previous nine years was so abusive in every way that she thought there was no escape and that even if she did, who would want her? My anxiety was through the roof, having depression combined with Complex Post Traumatic Stress Disorder, [c.p.t.s.d] to boot, and such low self-esteem it wasn't even funny. I just wanted it all to end.

Then I met Matt, and he and I became best friends. It was refreshing to have a conversation that wasn't a fight about what my now-ex wanted to spend money on. It was nice to have an intelligent conversation because Matt is a brilliant guy who liked most of my interests. He also appreciated my intelligence instead of belittling me for it or saying that I was using big words to make him feel stupid, as my ex would do to me repeatedly. Technically, I met him two years before I got to the point of wanting to give up, but knowing I couldn't because of my children. Well, in 2020, I finally got the courage to leave. I didn't know what I would do next, but I had faith that my best friend would help me as much as he could. That small glimmer of hope was more than enough to start over again.

That was June of 2020, and thankfully, my ex was in jail, so I was free to explore finding myself and learning to love myself again because to love others, you have to learn to love yourself truly; flaws and all. Matt allowed me to move in with him as I didn't have a job or place to go after leaving my ex. Some days, Matt would work all day and then stay up all night with me, just listening to me talk, helping me to enjoy music again. He showed me that I was worthy of respect and my feelings were valid, even if he didn't always agree. Then again, he had been hurt in his previous relationships and was guarded, too. It was during that time when I truly had one of the most beautiful and romantic nights of my life, there was nothing sexual about it. We just stayed up all night listening to music, using songs to tell each other how we truly felt about the other. I felt so beautiful and loved that night seeing myself through his eyes as he held me and sang to me and I did the same to him.

Soon after I freed myself from my ex, we became "friends with benefits, but monogamous." He made me feel beautiful and wanted in a way I had never felt before. We started falling in love with each other at that point. I won't lie to you; we both fought it as one. There is a seven-year age difference with me being older, and also, I have kids and am just getting out of a horrible nine-year relationship.

In August, Matt went to Texas with his family leaving me home alone. It was during the week of separation that we both finally accepted the fact that we wanted to be in a fully committed relationship with each other. When he came on August 3rd, he asked me, very adorably I might add, to become his girlfriend. I, of course, said yes, as I also wanted to be with him fully. It didn't matter that I was still incredibly broken. He didn't see someone who was broken and trash and deserved to be treated like a piece of trash meant to be used and tossed away like my ex made me believe for so long. Matt saw me as beautiful and deserving to be loved, and cherished and wanted me to be his life partner.

We became an official couple, and yes, we have had plenty of struggles, especially when it came to my ex. He was bound and determined to split us up, thinking that in doing so, I would return to him. He would use what he knew about me and my personality to try and make me betray Matt in any way possible. I never cheated on Matt, as I love him way too much. Fear, however, makes us do things we would never do, especially when trying to protect the ones we love the most. So building trust was very hard, especially when we both had trust issues. To begin with, both of us had been cheated on multiple times in the past. I didn't make it any easier, as I would keep things to myself; that self-preservation instinct was so firmly embedded in my psyche. It has taken a lot of work to break that, to fully let my guard down and be honest with Matt about everything going on with me, both in the past and present. And let's be honest, the relationship will fail if there is no trust. Amazingly, he was understanding and has stood by me through some of the worst times in my life and his.

I have tried to support him financially and emotionally as much as he has me. Yes, we fight; what couple doesn't? But we can talk it out and move forward. Yes, we both can, in the heat of the moment, bring up past hurts that we did to each other, but we are working on moving past them entirely. It's hard, especially when we see ourselves as damaged goods and unworthy of being loved, to accept the unconditional love we give each other.

There are times when we both have wanted to give up, that things felt like they were too much and too hard. The good times far outweigh the bad, and we stuck together to push through the pain and kept working together to grow as a couple and as individuals. I had so much work to do on myself to feel like I deserved the love and devotion this wonderful man gave me. He was able to see through my flaws. He supported me financially and emotionally in my journey to becoming "Crystal Phoenix," as I call myself on my speaking platform. I went through many different ideas of what I wanted to become until

I finally accepted that helping others and speaking up for those who feel they can't is my calling, and I've embraced it. He and I have had to start over, and that honestly has been the best thing for us, as we were able to break away from all the negative energy and people who wanted to see us fail and break up. In doing so, we have gotten back to the basics of a solid and loving relationship, where I feel more loved and beautiful than I have ever been.

So, as you can see, even though I saw myself as damaged goods, someone thought I was beautiful and worthy of being treated like the queen that I, in his eyes, am. In turn, I do my best to show him that he is worthy of unconditional love, very handsome, and wanted as well. Relationships can be challenging, but in the end, as long as you love and respect each other, there is nothing that you can't overcome together.

So here are a few ways that you can try to have what I have. First, learn to love yourself again, because honestly, you can't really love anyone unless you can love yourself. True happiness begins with you.

Second, start off building a true friendship first; don't just dive right in. Build a solid foundation and go from there. Forcing feelings just because you are attracted to someone, or they say all the right things does nothing but lead to heartache, trust me I know. Also, as much as I hate to admit it, having a rebound can be a healthy way to get over your abusive ex, but if you want to find true love, real love, I find it is best to be friends first and lovers second.

Third, don't look for it. When you are ready, they will come to you. I find myself saying that to so many people who say they have given up on finding anyone. Most of the time what you are looking for is already there and you don't even know it. They are just waiting for you to be ready for them. Usually it's that friend who has always been by your side no matter what, just waiting for you to see them as more than a friend. I mean look at me and Matt, we went from best friends to basically married, neither of us knowing that it would ever happen. So remember to keep your heart open to the good things in life because you never know when your soul mate will appear, if they haven't already.

I am a domestic abuse awareness advocate/speaker/author and recovery coach. My main focus is to change the way people think about victims of domestic abuse and help them go from surviving to thriving, rising out of the ashes like the Phoenix they truly are. I am a voice for those who feel silenced.

I dedicate this chapter to those who feel that they are damaged goods in hopes that I have shown you that you aren't. To my children because they are proof that no matter how broken we are you always can find a reason to love and finally to Matt who has given me more love and support and shown me that I am not damaged goods but a beautiful woman who deserves to be loved and cherished in and out of the bedroom.

It's in the Grey Zone We Find The Colors

By: Susannah Dawn

"I'm not what I used to be, yet I am who I've always been."
~ Susannah Dawn

Grey – a neutral color viewed as neither black nor white. The word conjures up a sense of walking through a thick fog or standing outside on a dismal winter's day that cannot decide if it wants to snow, rain... or something else. The sheer neutrality of the color lacks the vibrancy one can feel on a sunny spring day as the sun shines high in the sky, the birds sing, and the flowers are in full bloom. It's a color of hiding, like the grey-painted battleships that are less obvious to see on the high seas. Even the emotions associated with the color come across as solemn, quiet, and even dreary.

At the same time, we live in a world of absolutes, a place where people often view things as being black or white. Sure, there is color, but it loses its luster as others group people into boxes. Once they learn something about us, they use that small piece of knowledge to define who we are, and invariably place us in a box... with a label – often a stigma – to define how, or if, they will interact in a positive way. This is a true shame, as they fail to take any time to interact and get to know the real person. The imagined boxes we get placed in cannot define who we are, our authentic selves.

Unfortunately, people rationalize this process as how it must be, how it's the only way for our minds to quickly decide our impressions of others amidst all the information we gather daily. In doing so, they tend to focus on one slight aspect of a person and thereby judge them based on that one piece of information instead of seeing the person as a whole. They don't comprehend how such conduct may keep them from a business relationship, a friendship, that would be an abundant flower in their life. People may avoid the grey zone as a dreary place. Yet, at the same time, they turn the non-grey places into a darker wasteland filled with labeled boxes to give them an identity: business/job status, family role, financial situation, _____, etc.

As noted above, once some aspect about us is revealed, people place us in boxes, expanding the wasteland with labels and stigmas that are not likely to be glamorous: neurodiverse, overcome addiction, family situation, _____, etc. Thus, if one is neurodiverse –a wide spectrum in and of itself, they're unceremoniously placed in a box labeled neurodiverse. Any stigma towards that label is how the placer paints everybody within that box. While some may think it's colorful, it makes for a world that is more of a black-and-white organization.

We do this to ourselves, as well, usually by crawling into a box of imposter syndrome, being culturally different, having self-doubt, _____, etc. I also know of people who slip into the grey zones as a way to hide, thinking if they slide into that realm, it will be a haven where the drab ambiance will obscure them from the world... yet it's just another way to box one's self. All of this is why, in life, people feel they have a box to fill, a label to define them; if they don't like where they'd be placed, they try to hide their truth so others won't find out about it and thus "might" speak to or treat them differently.

Even though living a life in boxes may feel icky or stifling, it provides many people a sense that they have a role, a place in their families or communities, and thereby can avoid the grey zones. They see it as a place to fear, where they have no control over their lives... unfortunately, these same people fail to realize that, if they would only look in a mirror, that is the life they currently live.

However, where others see dreariness, I view the grey zone as a place of abundance and color... and the only place where I can thrive. It's the opposite of the "outside" world, where everyone wants to label and place others in boxes, where they identify as X or Y or ??? Inside the grey, one is not ruled by the societal norms of the world and doesn't have to limit themselves to what others expect – unless they so desire. There is freedom to "be" our authentic, amazing selves.

Remember, when there are so many aspects about us – all those different pieces of who we are, there will be many who decide that just one small piece – usually one they don't like – is the total sum of who we are... is all we are. They only treat us based on how they view anyone else with that trait – their view of that particular box. For them, placement in a box is not to live in the grey zone, for there is no grey about it. Being told this is what we are and where we're supposed to fit is actually black and white. Those closing us up in such containers have predetermined the definition of anyone in a specific box, including what and who they are, and have cherrypicked their example of what everyone in that confined space is like.

Yet for me... I don't fit any box, and I never did.

My personal story is an example of dealing with the boxes of others, being controlled by them until I realized there was no longer a need to listen to them. It was only when I stepped into the grey zone that it became possible for me to thrive. It was in that same space where I could finally see color, the true vivid spectrums of all colors around me, and the beautiful hearts and souls of the people who crossed my path. Within the grey zone, all limitations of boxes were neutralized.

However... it took time for that awareness to ignite inside me.

To better understand my story is to know the pain of

being told to be and live as something – someone – I wasn't. It began with my father, who would spank me if I showed any outward appearance other than his expectations. That was followed by his teasing and ridicule at moments throughout childhood that he chose to reinforce his expectation, which continued into high school when he shot down every idea I wanted to pursue, including career options... I wanted to be an astronomer, to which he replied there was no money or advancement and to stick with "safe" jobs with better pay and guaranteed advancement. That pain was further solidified by society and the expectations of following its standards or risk being harmed, which included mental, physical, and all points between.

As a child, my only option was to try and comply. However, consider how it would feel to crawl into a space in which it's clear you don't belong. This would reinforce your feeling of being an imposter and completely drain you, causing you to withdraw from everyone around you. That was my life.

To grasp my story better, you must also know this: my face is only three and a half years old.

For some, the comprehension of those words gave them an image in which they placed me in a box and immediately decided their opinion of me. They selected specific impressions from within that box to support how they view everyone in that space as the same. They don't know me, my story, or how I am more than all the boxes one could use to define me... nor do they care.

That's their loss, for I will continue to thrive in the grey zone.

Growing up, I knew who I was at my core... in my soul. It was clear to me by the age of three, and from that moment on, it never changed. Through every moment of every day of every year, I knew and understood exactly who I was at a very personal level that occurs between one's Creator and self. That knowledge and understanding never wavered; there was never a hesitation about who I am.

We are all created uniquely with different paths to follow through life. Consider how our stories are similar... the fears holding us back. The people in our lives telling us what to do when they don't understand (or care) that their control goes against what we're able to do because we're neurodiverse – diagnosed or not, overcame an addiction, have non-regional accents, and so many more. We get placed in many boxes, impacting how others view and treat us.

Unfortunately for me, it was my father who first forced me to be something I knew I wasn't. He only saw me as a shell, that visible piece of us that is the first thing people usually see when we meet. His expectation from my birth was to have a "little him" to carry on the family name and make him proud based on the shell encompassing my soul.

It wasn't gonna happen. As I mentioned before, I know who I am. It was so obvious to me that I went to bed at the age of three, praying to God every night to wake up and be treated as the girl I knew I was.

It wasn't my fault the Lord, in His infinite wisdom, placed me in a shell that didn't align with my soul. And once my father figured out that I was going down a path that would lead me to womanhood, once he caught me playing dress up with my mom's clothes, he spanked me. At first, I couldn't understand why he did that as he said nothing... just spanked me. From that point forward, if I were caught, spankings followed. Soon, he reinforced his message with teasing and ridicule. I was traumatized by emotional, psychological, and mental abuse by not be allowed to exhibit my true self.

The result was that I could not trust or feel safe with my family. Once I withdrew from my parents, pulling away from my friends followed, and then I retreated from society as it was not safe to be my authentic self during that era of history. I was being told to identify as a male, which felt wrong. At the same time, I never "identified" as female, either, although that was due to knowing at my core I was female. So, trying to appease family and society, I tried to identify as a shell I never liked. True, it was because of that shell I accomplished things I'd have never been able to do had God put me in a shell that aligned with who I am. He had a purpose for this, to include my time in the US Army. It's a piece of me.... a career as a cavalry officer is a piece of who I am. God knew I had to go through the pain of living as a shell – I would have moments when the pain was so unbearable that I wished myself out of existence, to die – before I could finally live authentically as the amazing woman in my soul, He created me to be.

If you hadn't guessed, Faith is my foundation. I was blessed with a miracle after almost a half century of life, when the Lord opened doors to let me be me in this world. Through that, He helped me regain the confidence I'd lost in childhood. People showed up along my path I never expected, beautiful souls who were there for specific purposes, including the amazing group of sisters I now find around and supporting me. It included Him igniting my awareness of the boxes I'd tried to contort myself to fit... in which I never could fit or belong, with an ability to see my path from new viewpoints beyond where I've felt stuck.

Yes... it all comes back to those pesky boxes. Someone who reads my story might put me into an LGBTQ box. Another might find out I've had issues with impostor syndrome my whole life, including trying to identify as someone I'm not, and put me in a different box focused on that. Another learns I was a cavalry officer, and suddenly that becomes my box. And so on and so on... with each placement done with a specific narrative view of everyone within that box.

So, what does it mean to thrive in the grey zone?

One way is to understand that there are times when those in our situation are NOT the right ones to connect with. Once someone learns a certain part of my story, they often offer to introduce me to people they know. Not being one to turn down potential connections and hopeful future collaborators, I accept, only to find they've selected people from a specific group I never felt a connection with just because of a sliver of who I am. When they find out my true self doesn't align with my shell, they assume I want to meet similar people, yet those introductions usually turn sour quickly as I feel no connection with them and no sense of belonging.

Think of a person, we'll call her Judy, who could be viewed as being part of a group inside Box A. Within that box is a diverse group of people, not unlike the diversity of the country itself. Judy could be viewed as part of a small sub-group of people in the box, yet feels no connection to them or anyone in the box as a whole. However, she's only funneled to meet people in Box A because those doing the connecting seem to think that, if her _____ places her inside that box, then she must obviously want to connect with anyone in that box – since they're all viewed as being the same. However, Judy feels no sense of belonging – or safety – in that box or with that group... has never seen herself as part of that community.

This is why it's important to know yourself FIRST, no matter where you are. My best friends in first and second grade were girls, and I've always felt aligned with the girls in my classes and the amazing women who entered my life in recent years. In middle school, I had a vision of how women were so much more capable; once I was living authentically, my purpose was to work with other women so we could all soar. This includes helping those who feel stuck in life to ignite their awareness and move beyond those places – boxes – to take back control of their lives.

You may be confused about your place in this world, yet know what you both want and can do. When your awareness is ignited, you begin to see how not only are you stuck in a box of some type, but who – or what – is in control becomes visible. This is where the excitement begins. You realize how you can take that control back, step up, and say, *"This is me. This is who I am. I'm done letting these characters rule my life. I'm taking back my life and control of it, and will move beyond this box. And once I'm beyond its walls, I'm going to live – and thrive – in the grey zone."*

And here's another thing... the grey zone is where the most vibrant colors are located, meaning it's not grey.

Although it's our experiences in life that shape us, our core doesn't change... ever. However, we constantly live through changes – reinvention – which create new experiences. So, while our authentic self remains constant, life's events are what take us through our changes. It's because of those experiences we're often placed in a box. We're placed in a space where we know we don't belong, where others placed us because that's where / how they view us. We can also put ourselves in boxes, like impostor syndrome, or we listen to society and accept what it might say about some small piece of us as able to define us. Remember: it's only a piece.

It's time to stop holding onto the pains received from others. The longer we hold them, the stronger and heavier the anchor to our past becomes, pulling us underwater. It keeps us focused on our past, on our pains, so we only look behind us when we need to live in the present to thrive. When we focus on the past, it's likely to become our future, whereas living in the now, accepting others for who they are, forgiving those who harmed us, and not holding grudges allows us to cut those chains and let them and the pains of the past quietly slip below the waves.

We are all created to be unique, for there will never be another you – or me – in this world. By staying stuck, you deprive the world of the amazing person you were meant to be, placed here specifically at this moment in time to help lift others in positive ways. If you feel the path before you is daunting, believe it's safer to hide in your shell – your box, and understand that your journey does not require you to walk it alone.

The only reason I'm here at this moment to write this chapter is that I recognized that I didn't need to walk this journey alone. I accepted those sent to walk with and support me when my own family rejected me. You must do the same, for we only have this one lifetime to accomplish our purpose.

Susannah Dawn no longer fits the proverbial box – and never did. Having entered 2022 with a total reinvention, she now looks at life and business from a vantage point set beyond labels... beyond boxes... those places in which our fears work hard to confine us, keeping us from seeing how we are so much more than boxes and labels could ever express.

Susannah speaks at length on the importance of women being our authentic selves... of moving past the fears and self-doubt holding us back from success... and thereby turn the obstacles of pivoting – of the reinvention process, into speed bumps. Susannah's goal is to lift other women to step beyond their own boxes... and shine.

Susannah is a 4-time International Bestselling Author, is a featured entrepreneur in premium global journal articles, and her "Armor of God" fantasy series is an example of a journey beyond boxes. Her website is www.SusannahDawnWriter.com.

When I think about family, those close to me from whom I felt unconditional love and support, the first person I turn to is a sister I chose – and who chose me... who I never knew until one year ago: CJ... you know her as Dr. Constance Leyland. There was an instant connection during our first Zoom chat. She's the first person I felt truly safe to open up to, and tell all parts of my story knowing there was no judgment. We met IRL after she asked me to go with her to an event across the country, and with her I broke most of the remaining walls around me. She was the first, though now that group of sisters has grown to include Christine, Danielle, Kirsten, and Nhu. And... I honestly know that I would not be here if not for my sisters. I love you all.

The Odyssey of Shades to Self-Discovery

by: Mike Ashabraner

This chapter serves as an empowering guide for those who find themselves in unexpected leadership roles, offering practical advice on navigating the complexities and uncertainties of leadership with confidence and authenticity. I am an unintended leader myself, sharing my journey from confusion and self-doubt to becoming a purpose-driven leader capable of inspiring and guiding others through their challenges. I emphasize the importance of connecting to one's inner compass and strength, leveraging personal challenges as opportunities for growth and self-discovery.

Numerous individuals find themselves in leadership roles without having actively sought them out. This phenomenon refers to those who unexpectedly become leaders, assuming positions of influence and becoming a beacon for others in search of direction. If this resonates with you, you're not alone. While there's an abundance of guidance for individuals who aspire to leadership, resources can seem scarce for those thrust into these roles unprepared. This chapter aims to bridge that gap, offering practical advice and strategies to navigate leadership's unforeseen challenges and complexities, ensuring you're equipped to steer through any storm with confidence and skill.

Why listen to me?

Because I was an unexpected leader who found myself in some pretty tough situations, I wasn't prepared for it at the outset. However, by connecting to my inner compass and strength, I was not only able to rise to the occasion, but I was also able to embrace the natural-born leader within me. Challenges are a part of life, and no one is immune to their effects.

But only 5% of people who go through challenging circumstances use the experience to build their dream life. That's what I've been doing and why I wrote this chapter for you. Yes, there's inspiration here. There's also real guidance for your journey into being your best self, regardless of what's going on in your life right now. No bullshit, no fluff. Just concrete real-world experience from one unexpected leader to another.

So how did I get here?

When I was starting out, I was all passion and no clue. Now I am all passion with *some* clue and with the right community support. I've built the Hounds Of Business Community. It's the best place for heart-centered people to grow and thrive in business by linking arms with like-minded people for success. Many of our members were people who struggled with finding their inner leader and building their purpose-led businesses. But through the support of our community, they've become more empowered and enabled to lead others through their journey.

Remember, there is always light at the end of the tunnel

We often fixate on external factors and outcomes beyond our control, overlooking our power to shape responses to life's events. I aim to shift your focus towards what's within your grasp—your reactions and adherence to personal values amidst life's tumults. Life presents defining moments that can alter our path, presenting us with the tough choice between succumbing to defeat or summoning the courage to press on. Recently, I faced such a crossroads, a daunting challenge that made quitting seem appealing. But remember, entertaining the thought of giving up doesn't signify weakness; rather, your resilience is defined by how you tackle these moments. Choosing to persevere, leveraging inner strength over fear, loss, and uncertainty, underscores our true fortitude.

We often fixate on external factors and outcomes beyond our control, overlooking our power to shape responses to life's events. I aim to shift your focus towards what's within your grasp—your reactions and adherence to personal values amidst life's tumults. Life presents defining moments that can alter our path, presenting us with the tough choice between succumbing to defeat or summoning the courage to press on. Recently, I faced such a crossroads, a daunting challenge that made quitting seem appealing. But remember, entertaining the thought of giving up doesn't signify weakness; rather, your resilience is defined by how you tackle these moments. Choosing to persevere, leveraging inner strength over fear, loss, and uncertainty, underscores our true fortitude.

Embrace this core truth

Life exists in the gray zone, not in the black and white. We're all trying to get out of the gray. But it's in the gray is where you truly find yourself. That's a big life lesson I've learned as I've journeyed from being in the fire department to working with nonprofits and now to now leading the Hounds Of Business Community.

Each step along the way has had all sorts of polarizing moments. Though I might not have enjoyed it at the time, I needed each one of them to help clear the muck and the mire away from my understanding of who I really am. Getting through the fears and the doubts to embrace myself in a different way has taken me out of the cloudiness of the gray and into the brightness of the sun. In this process, I've learned that nothing is ever between me and someone else. It is always between me and God.

Here's my story, can you relate?

The first thing to know about me is that I'm a people-first person. Always have been. Since I am completely open and vulnerable here, I used to be a people-pleaser. My time in the fire department was all about that. I joined at age eighteen because I wanted to be somebody and do something special with my life.

Growing up in a very unstable home with an abusive, alcoholic parent did not provide much guidance in fostering inner peace and confidence. Looking back, it seems that the lack of strong roots, not feeling grounded, or confident in who I am, made my life a constant struggle for validation and inner peace.

I didn't know at the time that there were some core values that guided me along the way. Although I didn't have ideal relationships and didn't love myself much, I was blessed to have amazing grandparents. They provided me with an alternative example of stability, love, and strong family values. I guess you could say they planted the seeds in me of honor, integrity, commitment, and empathy. Those seem to be the definition of what drives my core values today as a man and leader.

This is why legends like King Arthur, Sun Tzu and Augustus Caesar have shaped who I am and what I've created in life and business. I subconsciously sought to do just as Gandhi instructed us, "Be the change you want to see in the world."

For the first 38 years of my life, I took Ghandi's words literally. I always sought to find my place in the world and to discover my own happiness and inner peace but never found it. You see, I was always searching for those character traits in external people and circumstances. Until recently.

The story of The Hounds of Business

In December 2022, the pandemic severely disrupted

my financial business and its expansion, including a subsidiary operation supporting other financial executives. The restrictions meant the end of in-person networking and collaboration, crucial elements for my business's growth, leading to a significant setback.

Adapting to the circumstances, I turned to social media, primarily LinkedIn, to sustain my business. However, lacking a solid strategy, I found myself engaging in ineffective outreach, commonly known as "pitch-slapping," which likely annoyed many users. This phase of trial and error became a humorous anecdote, attributing my receding hairline to the stress caused by these social media endeavors, half-jokingly blaming it on the intense online engagement initiated by my attempts to navigate digital networking.

On that long cold December night, I met a crazy cage fighter from Chicago, who was a social media influencer. For months I'd seen his posts and really liked what I saw then one day he reached out to me. It reminded me of the scene from The Wizard of Oz, where they pull the curtain back and expose who the wizard really was. He texted me so many enlightening, life-changing things that I sat outside for 3 hours asking him questions and getting every piece of helpful information I could.

What he said was life changing because it hit me at my core. For the first time someone was affirming that all I wanted to be and see to change the world was actually possible. Not only was it possible it was doable! How did I know that? Because he was doing it.

During a reflective conversation on a chilly December night, we delved into topics deeply rooted in my innermost self. We discussed the art of drawing others in, cultivating meaningful connections, and establishing supportive environments that facilitate a culture of familiarity, respect, and trust.

Remember, deep down I always wanted to believe that I was someone. That all of my terrible challenges and life experiences had a higher purpose. That if people got to see me and my heart that they would know, like, and trust me. And if I could get people to know, like, and trust me for who I am at the core, then maybe I could support them to leave a legacy in their life and business.

Little did I know that this life-changing event would do just that

So that very December night, I joined that cage fighter on LinkedIn among other folks like me who were also trying to figure out how to be seen and grow their businesses. I watched and observed how he was able to inspire people to have courage before confidence, get unstuck and take the first baby steps to living a rewarding and fulfilling life. The way he spoke with confidence was undeniable and exactly what I wanted for my own life.

About three months later, he asked me the most profound and life-changing questions I had ever heard. He called me out of the blue and said, "Your LinkedIn profile sucks. You're wearing a suit in your picture. Why?"

What the...? "Because I'm a fiduciary. In the financial industry, we are expected to take a bath, dress nicely, and speak properly to show authority with our knowledge," I replied sarcastically yet honestly.

To which he asked, "Is that working for you? " And my answer was a resounding, "HELL NO! I would make more money recycling tin cans right now."

Then he went on to say that I'm a working class, down-to-earth kinda-guy, that I should lean into that, be myself and let my unfiltered redneck self out for the world to see and experience. "But I can't do that. I'll be a laughingstock. It will never work," I tried to deny and counter.

"But is it working now?"

"Hell, no it's not working now," I whined.

"So, what do you have to lose?"

Wow! Those three questions were the most life-changing questions that I've ever experienced. For the very first time I had the courage to dig deep into my inner self, not external circumstances or seeking validation from others. I had to do the hardest work any human being can do: the inner journey into what we bury in the subconscious. Because that's where the pain resides in all of us.

On that very day I said to myself, "To hell with it. I want to be happy. I want to define who I am and what success means to me, not what I've been told it should mean for the last forty years!". It's like I always say when it comes to owning your authenticity, "You can spray Lysol on a dog turd, but it's still a dog turd." So, just be yourself.

That's what led me to put on my favorite camo hat, dust off my flannel shirt, and journey down the path to self-discovery for the very first time. Four months later in April, I began to abandon all of the crazy sales pitches and stuff we were told to do in business to earn money. Rather, I set out to define who I am and what I truly wanted to do, be, and accomplish in life. I started to see things like rejection much differently. I saw it as an opportunity to dig deep and to learn and grow from it. From a place of inner awareness, I was able to use my extremely high EQ to relate to the pain and struggles of others and foster life changing relationships with them.

I was attracting people that were just like me at heart-level and in the same phase of life. I met someone who became a great friend and trusted confidant in business, who gave me the affirmation and certainty as I began to build the Hounds of Business Community. An online community that I surprisingly created without trying to and couldn't have done alone.

We connected on a heart level because of where we were both at in life. She was going through a lot, left a job, and had just started her own business. Instead of trying to sell my business services to her, I decided to connect her with other good people I had met on LinkedIn and to help her all I could through my recent networking experiences online.

My only goal was to use my life and business experiences, pain, struggles and the wisdom I had gained from it to help her and others regain her confidence quicker, learn more about sales and marketing, and to be successful. I knew deep down that if people could see my heart and my intention, that I may gain not only friends, but also clients.

Instead of trying to help her with finance, I helped her with learning how to effectively network and grow on LinkedIn . I recognized that I was a few steps ahead and wanted to help her avoid the struggles and lack of confidence and uncertainty that often comes with starting and growing a business, in any way I could. Looking back, I did help her, as the first of many, in extraordinarily life-changing ways. The ROI when serving people isn't always tangible. We can help each other with each phase of business and be supportive friends for confidence and self-assurance to grow and flourish.

How do you measure affirmation, confidence, certainty? And how do you quantify knowing that, for the first time in my life, I am not crazy or full of shit? Knowing that all of the sad struggles and unfortunate things I've learned in my life could be used to change someone else's life and business still amazes me.

It changed me from the inside out.

Without that affirmation, I would not have kept going to help hundreds more people get unstuck, feel like they belong and have the courage to journey to a place of passion and purpose. It's how I learned a valuable lesson: Manage business but lead people. That experience flourished into multiple experiences with amazing people that have been worn down and fatigued in life and business, just as I had been. It led to the creation of The Hounds Of Business Community.

We started as a group of friends from all walks of life who helped each other grow after struggling to understand ourselves, life and business. Now, we are a group of businesspeople that rapidly become friends because we share the desire to build successful purpose led businesses and are passionate about creating legacies.

Today, we help businesspeople increase their net worth, by tapping into our network. We are an International Business Hub and Resource Bank that can help businesses from all industries and from startups to multi-million dollar corporations. Social media is a rented and competitive space where we can get kicked off for little reason and we are lost in a sea of looking like everyone else. The Hounds of Business provides the ecosystem to foster "Know, Like, And Trust" with your ideal clients and business partners that lead to more results. Think about it, who are you likely to do business with…a random person you don't know, or someone you "know, like, and trust" and has helped you out for months?

Some Redneck Life & Business Lessons to Remember

Several months after putting the Hounds together, I grew the community to about forty active professionals without ever talking about my financial business. That is until the market changed and those people reached out to me for help. To say I was pleasantly surprised is an understatement. I spent months helping people on LinkedIn grow their confidence and feel special.

They know what the next steps to take in business without me ever talking about finance. That is when I learned a valuable life lesson, which is one of the Hounds Pack Principles: *Attract like a bug zapper and stop being a dog catcher.*

Think about it. If you chase something that doesn't want to be caught, what does it usually do? It runs away faster. That is how I view traditional sales and marketing. It is a hunter mentality and puts us in a position to be constantly chasing something we will never catch. And it's why pitch-slapping just doesn't work in business, especially on LinkedIn.

Contrast that with a bug zapper. It just sits there never moving and things fly into it all night long. For me, I have little convincing and persuasion skills with direct sales. Plus, I hate it. But what I can do is foster/nurture a deep level of trust with the right people. Giving them such tremendous value that leads to them choosing to work with me on their own, they also become fierce advocates and send others to me for help as well.

So, tell me. Who is going to pass up on the opportunity to get clients now, clients in the future, and a network of advocates that send you both? Whoever gets to the dog bowl first, eats first. No one. That's who. This is why for the past two years my mantra has been this: find Joe Rogan and Oprah *before* they became the successful icons that we know of today.

Think about it. Everyone in every industry thinks that to be successful, they need to network with the biggest names in the game. That's why they're all trying to work with Joe Rogan/ Oprah level professionals. Like that legendary game changer asked me, "How's that working out for you?" It seems out of my league and too exhausting for a country boy working out of his office shed to try and link up with Joe Rogan or someone similar to grow my business on LinkedIn.

That's where being authentic, building genuine connections with people, being heart-centered instead of only profit-focused, and helping people first leads to wins for everyone involved. Unexpected leadership requires you to think differently than everyone else does. Because let's just be real here, everyone has been screwed by someone and most people don't trust anyone. Especially on social media where charlatans and fakers are constantly trying to sell us their programs, but don't actually care about our success or future.

You don't have to fit into someone else's box or criteria to be successful and find the right people for you to grow. My story is proof of that. The life lesson here is to change the way you look at yourself and the outside world. Choose yourself first. Or to say it another way, stop being a dog that is trying to meow because someone told you to. Just become the best dog you can be, bark proudly, and own it. Remember, you can spray Lysol on a dog turd, but it is still a dog turd. When you choose to do that inner journey to find yourself and embrace your authenticity, you'll find everything you need to be able to link up with the right people and grow.

Here's a short breakdown of some key takeaways to have confidence and move forward through the gray zone of unexpected challenges:

1. Only you get to define who you are/who you want to be and define success on your own terms.
2. What others call weird or quirky are actually your greatest superpowers.
3. Guard your thoughts and what you accept as truth. It is like not putting rat poison in your food pantry.
4. Explore life, put yourself out there for God and the universe to bring opportunities to you as you test

out your superpowers with childlike wonder.

5. Surround yourself with mature people that appreciate your value and express it through reciprocity.
6. Take your business and mission seriously, just not yourself seriously.

This is how you become a key person of transformation, whether you're an unexpected leader or an intentional one. You become that key person who influences others to be their best self and change the world.

I dedicate this chapter to my beautiful wife and two amazing daughters, that kept me going when I probably wouldn't have. Shout out to my man and master storyteller, D. Grant Smith for helping me turn my rumbly thoughts into this!

Mike Ashabraner, RedneckFinancialCoach.com

Mike Ashabraner, known as the Redneck Financial Coach, is a testament to resilience and the power of community. Rising from the hardships of poverty in Kentucky, Mike faced bankruptcy in 2010 but transformed his life with the help of a mentor. Embracing his knack for uniting people and offering down-to-earth financial advice, he became a beloved financial coach. His unique approach and relatable 'redneck' persona led to the rapid growth of his business and the birth of the Hounds of Business community. Today, Mike is an acclaimed advisor, helping entrepreneurs enhance their net worth with his unconventional wisdom, Hound Pack Principles, and a network that fosters immediate connections. His story, marked by his iconic camouflage cap and memorable country proverbs, inspires many to navigate their financial journeys with courage and authenticity.

How I found my inner light through darkness

By: Olivier Dierickx

Welc'Home everyone to my story, kind of few pralines to taste aside dozens of others in a heavy box. I feel so honored to be beside 20+ other authors who came through their journey alive, sharing their stories. May you be inspired by what we unfold here. Each title word is written in French. Feel free to stay until the end, I have special extra pralines for you! This chapter is just a glimpse of a whole universe to discover.

As you may realize, I am creative with my words and you will find these treats within my chapter. This is the way I use to give my life a meaning. However, writing is a challenge for me, as my inner monkey mind often jumps in to tell me to do other things. I might tell you this later, yet I want to let you know you are deeply loved and seen as a beautiful soul. Your presence matters. We are all loved as we are.

I wish I would have had someone tell me that 30+ years ago when I faced the darkest moments of my life. Or that I had an imaginary friend like Marnie to help me navigate in stormy seas. I'm glad I survived to share what I endured. I don't wish anyone else on Earth to live through what I lived, though it still happens and will sadly always happen. I truly believe there's no fate but what we do on a daily basis.

We also need more love, kindness, and self-love classes at schools, and Angels in human bodies. Though we do not all perceive, yet there are thousands of beings that love us even more than we do ourselves.

Bonjour!

Hello!... *"Is it me you're looking for?"* It was certainly not the first word that came into my mouth when I was delivered by my mom on this Earth, yet it was for sure the word that was spoken to me the most by my dad, mom, family, and friends that surrounded this amazing Angel smiling cutie baby that I was. My presence, even within an imperfect and flawed body was, and still is today, a miracle of God.

Before I water the seeds of my Poe-Tree story in this anthology and before I pay gratitude to many other humans that took part in my journey and transformed my life, I want to heartly thank the two astounding human beings that helped me to survive and navigate until today: my mom Lucie and my dad Edgard.

I would like first to show you the soil. I was born within a country that stretches between France, the Netherlands, Luxembourg and Germany: Belgium! This country was built on successive migrants who brought their cultures, languages, food and music. Now you know where my passion comes from!

For almost 200 years, this country had to navigate between forces while fighting for its independence. My ancestors endured WWI and WWII. God bless the next generations in Europe that didn't have to face any other global wars, until now.

My granddad never told me what happened to him, yet he was deported during WWII. The only way it made sense to me, once I knew, were some German words he taught me. My heart is deeply craving to see no more wars occur, as it creates trauma effects years after, and even beyond generations. Would we have enough strength as individuals to stop this cycle from repeating, to see humanity really thrive?

From my mom's side, having just my grandparents and a sole uncle, and my life chapter with them was sadly closed when I was 30 years old. From my dad's side, having five uncles and aunties and dozens of cousins. I still now have some kind of relationship with very few of them. I don't have any grandparents alive anymore for fifteen years... I don't push any more doors, the definition of family changed.

Olivier

So here I am. What a start to my adventure it was, for me and my parents, on one of the hottest days of the 20th century, on the Summer solstice during the Dragon year, bringing the music of my heartbeat LIVE as a Gemini! They named me Olivier – which is pronounced Oli-Vee-Yay. I was certainly their Olive tree, the seed of peace in their union. Upon my deliverance on Earth, they already knew I would be their only child.

I spent my youth in the Ardennes, happy to see my grandparents, uncles and aunties, and cousins. And though there was something a bit odd, challenging, that I didn't understand until later in life, I was loved as a child and adolescent.

My parents did their best to help me to navigate through the challenges of my body, having multiple operations for my eyes, stomach, appendicitis, and other health issues. There were also challenges in my family. Few events happened during my childhood that transformed my path and growth for years and decades.

I'm glad I was able to see beyond these challenges. It was a painful process, but I found strength within me to seek the gold, and mend the pieces and make peace, as the Kintsugi Oli you see today (*Japanese art ceramic repair*).

Unique

Each moment of my journey is **unique**, as are yours. How to approach my youth, childhood and adolescence in a few lines while it could be expressed in a few books? It is as hard to summarize as it was hard to live these times. Let me try my best.

"In this world, there is an invisible magic circle. There's an inside and an outside. These people are inside. And I'm outside. It doesn't really matter."

This quote is from "When Marnie was There." My life looked similar to Anna, the character of this anime story. I can totally relate as I was, myself, too many years outside this circle, in my own prison of silence. So shocked by what I was living inside, and so disturbed by what I experienced at school, not finding any meaning, that I thought the best I could do was to silence my voice. Yet, my body had to speak.

Between the physical challenges of my body, my mom's illness and transition, my bullying moments at school, my grandparent's behavior towards my parents and uncle, you wouldn't probably have liked the Olivier you were seeing at that time, but if only a 'Marnie' was there for him 35 years ago...

It all came to a crescendo since my childhood. There were signs, though not ones that I could understand. The first was an argument between my dad and my mom. Well, it really wasn't, yet that was what I perceived as a child. The table was upside down, and all the veggies and plates were on the ground. I was terrified, I sought and found love, kindness and support from my neighbors.

It would be years later before I learned the truth. What I thought was an argument was an epilepsy crisis of my mom. However, as a child, I had my own questions. Was I the cause of their argument? Am I loved?

A few years later, we moved from the Ardennes to Brussels, where my mom found a job as a concierge in an office building. It was a lovely place with a pond, and located near a freeway.

I have fond memories with my grandmother during that time, fixing the wings of a bird, and of my first computer, having great moments with my Apple IIc! But the light would fade to darkness.

Within four years, my heart was hurt by things I didn't quite understand. First, my cute little dog, Dolly, became too curious to explore as she found her way to the freeway where her life ended. Then, my mom gradually lost her motricity.

One day, when I was alone with her, she attempted to stand up from the sofa. When she fell... I was petrified. I wasn't even able to move to help her.

Also, in his attempt to try his best, my dad was exhausted. They came to envision brain surgery for her. Challenges after challenges, my heart was wounded, especially since I had to see my mom without her long beautiful hair.

Nu

I didn't see any hope or improvement concerning my mom's health. On May 8th, 35 years ago, I left school at noon to be with my dad. We sat on a bench, and that was when he told me I would never see my mom again. We cried together, side by side, alone in our silence. This was the end. The end of our chapters with my mom. It was also the end of his suffering, as he would later tell me it was not the five years I was aware of, but much longer that she was ill.

I felt **naked**. My heart was in pieces. After that, I had great memories of 5 weeks of well deserved holidays in Yugoslavia (still a united country at that time), yet it was not enough to fill the void of the absence of my mom.

Following that tragedy, I had to live and endure two years in a foreign place, in a boarding school, only able to see my dad on weekends. Early on in life, I was already facing bullying at school.

However, those two years were as damaging for my heart as the Battle of Waterloo (which happened to be where my boarding school was). During my childhood, a group of children tried to force me to eat a fake rubber poop.

Yet during my time at boarding school, many other challenges came. Not only did I deal with the absence of my dad during the week, it was necessary to navigate within an environment where we were 6-12 adolescents per bedroom, with lockers.

Access was controlled to the shared showers, which were very hot in the evening, very cold in the early morning, and lacked intimacy. Then there was my facing bullying and mockery of all sorts, leaving no quiet time to be alone.

Déchiré

Every Friday I was happy to see my dad. And Sunday evening became my worst time, because I knew what would happen the next day. He would drive me back to Waterloo, letting me face my own Battles alone. Then came a particular night, the ultimate challenge I had to face.

And this time it was enough. I had ENOUGH!

Even today I don't talk often about that night, but it was pivotal and it took me years, even more than one or two decades, to heal from that event. It was something I was no longer able to handle as an adolescent, hurting my intimacy boundaries.

This particular night came certainly after difficult days or weeks, at school or within the boarding school. It doesn't really matter. All I remember is that I was so sad, depressed, and in my bed I was trying to give me some comfort. In my own bubble, I totally forgot that my environment was a room full of other adolescents, and one of them found the great idea to open the light and to joke at me, and others laughed at me.

Previously, I was doing things because my body had to express while my voice was silent. The message was "I am here, please see me". Whether it was at school to close a door that opens hardly (and got punished), or sadly, to end the life of a canary bird. But this time I didn't know how to deal with this. I was totally **torn**!

This event was way more than a shame for me. It was the final shutdown. The end of the relationship between my brain and my heart, between me and my body. It was the final hit, that this space is not safe anymore for me to express. To be ME.

Naturally, after my mom transitioned, my school results were not so good. My dad did the best he could but my recent times at boarding school were a disaster. He later found that the professional school was the best solution.

Even though there were computer classes (I have fond memories), these times were not conducive for me to improve. After failing four years in a row, I left school at 4th grade at 19 years old. French, biology, Latin, computers and photography were the only topics that I liked during my entire school years.

I then lived nearly 20 years of my life between alimentary jobs and unemployment times, navigating between the transition of my grandparents, my two cousins, my godfather, my dad's partner, my uncle and auntie, and recently a few friends.

After this event at boarding school, that truly was tearing my heart and my soul, I evolved disconnected. I tried to heal my broken heart, without any success.

I wasn't sad all the time, I had great moments, but since my adolescence I came through life without loving anyone for decades. Even not loving myself truly.

I'm glad I survived to tell my story. It wasn't the case of my cousin, Jérôme, who took his life more than 25 years ago, after a bike accident and an event that he wasn't able to cope with, that I will unfold in other time.

Alfred

As I navigate now towards the end, you may have noticed how the sections become the acronym. BOUNDARIES. Who better to illustrate this word than my uncle, who was not at all setting them, due to a toxic family.

Alfred is my Godfather and transitioned 18 years ago. His life, my relationship with him, always in the presence of my grandparents, and his transition, are an example of what happens when someone is not strong enough to set boundaries. Now it makes sense to me: he was trafficked by his parents.

My mom and he were the only children of my grandparents. And I was their only grandchild. My dad married my mom, that made my granddad pissed off, yet Alfred was alone with them. He tried to build his own life and even envisioned a marriage... which was canceled by my grandparents!

Eternally single, he found refuge in alcoholism. After my grandfather passed away, he took care of my grandmother until her transition seven years later. Following that, nearly four years of depression and solitude, not asking for help neither to me, my dad or anyone. I will not go further in the story, but his last years of life were sad.

Réouverture (puis déchirure)

There was frustration of living a major part of my life, feeling incomplete, and believing that I had lost 20+ years. Now I want to bring some light this time.

After years of solitude, I finally found love with a woman, at 36 years old. It was more than 10 years ago now, and lasted only 30 months, so after the **re-opening** of my heart with her, it was **torn again**. Later on I realized how precious the moments were.
"So if you cannot take my hand. And if you must be going. I will understand."
(from Make your own kind of music, Cass Elliot)

I wouldn't change these moments, because it wasn't until now, the only moments that I came finally to love someone, and after the breakup, to love me more than anyone else. It is an ongoing process not a checkbox. Some days I fail, some days I win.

Illuminer

We are here for a limited time on Earth. Billions of cells forming a small body that will finally set our soul free, letting the other billions of humans continue their lives until it's their turn. It might take years, sometimes decades, for some of us to awaken, yet when it's the case, it's our mission to **enlighten** this world. As I turn double-24 this year, I wish I will have 48 more years to live, yet it could be 48 weeks, or 48 days...

So, I urge you, my friends. Enjoy each drop of life. Don't delay your joy! And help each other around. We are truly not there to face it all alone. Feel your body!

Edgard

I want to find enough space to pay gratitude to my dad for the life he lived. This year he will turn 75, and his journey is a blessed example of resilience and humanity. Doing his best with what he had, he preserved me from his own hardships.

Even though we were fighting in silence with each other for decades, I came back to peace with him, especially after I decided to fly on my own, after 38 years of daily presence with him. As I know his years are counted, I enjoy his presence even more now than in the past.

Sacré

As this chapter is ending, I am... Relieved. My hope is that you feel less alone, and more loved. No matter what happens in our lives, we face all different kinds of struggles. We each have a story to tell, and often, they need to be heard by others to help them survive and thrive. If our stories could save the lives of hundreds of humans, then we can feel at peace when our last breath goes. Bring your own colors!

I truly believe this life is **Sacred**. That's why Olivier became Oli last year. After all that happened, I am now free of any box, any label. I am... Me. I am a soul in a human vehicle... a light being... alchemizing my traumas to become more human.

Whether you accept me as I am or not, I wish you peace. And I wish you to find your true sacred self. Thanks to all of us! This world needs more humanity.

Oli Dierickx is a NeuroLanguage coach and helps you to connect your heart with your brain when you learn and speak French. Passionate about languages, cultures, nature, and mental health, Oli is growing through authentic human connections.

Dedicated to my past versions, my parents Lucie and Edgard, Jérôme, Alfred, Angèle, Elif, Grace, Dorothy and Rachel. Their presence, life, guidance, and transition for Lucie, Jérôme, Alfred, Angèle and Dorothy, shaped the Oli you see today. Gratitude also to Dr Constance Leyland and the communities around her!

Dedicated also to the children and adolescents who are facing bullying, violence, trafficking, resulting to huge mental health challenges, leading sometimes to suicide. May they find persons like Marnie to help them to navigate into a world which needs them alive so they can level up humanity with their light, presence and actions.

You can find an extended and creative version of this chapter here:
https://linktr.ee/OliBeyondBoundaries

The "tail" of my Healing Heart

By: Isabelle Fortin

It was another beautiful Fall day. A cool breeze, and just a few clouds in the sky. I was a happy go lucky little girl, always laughing and spending most of my time outside. That was where I had spent the better part of that afternoon, completely oblivious of just how much my life was about to change.

For the past week, there had been a lot of people in the house. I now had to share my older sister's twin bed, and I was sick of it. I usually liked having company over, but they never stayed this long. Our house had always been the focal point of the family because of its central location, so every Christmas and Easter gathering would always happen at our home. But now it was dragging on and on, people would not leave and I didn't understand why.

It was Tuesday. I remember that detail because my favorite TV show was playing when my dad came home. As soon as he walked in, my sister got up and turned off the television. I remember thinking: *"How dare she turn off my favorite show?"* When I went to argue with her, my favorite aunt, Margo, looked at me with the kindest grin and asked me to please keep quiet.

My dad kneeled down in the middle of the living room with his face in his hands. I knew it was serious because he was sobbing, and my dad never cried. I had actually never seen my dad cry before that day!

When he regained his composure, he raised his head up, looked at my sister, my brother, and me, and said: *"Your mother died this afternoon."*

My mother was thirty-six.
I was five.

For a lack of a better way to explain it, they told me my mother was sleeping. I don't blame them! How would you explain death to a child? The truth is, there is no right way. Unfortunately, I would spend the next three-and-a-half decades afraid to sleep.

Overnight, I became a sad child, overwhelmed with grief. I didn't yet possess the tools to deal with any of this. The happy-go-lucky little girl I once was had died with her mother. I stopped smiling, would barely eat, and became desperate for love and affection. I was now just the shell of who I had been... of who I was meant to be.

The sad little girl soon became an extremely angry teenager. Anger was a much easier emotion to deal with. There's power in anger. To this day, I still don't understand how I never fell into drugs. I contemplated suicide on a daily basis. I didn't want to die; I only wanted the sadness to stop once and for all. But I could never do that to my dad! After all, he was grieving the loss of the love of his life.

My mother's death created a bottomless well of pain in my heart. It was a well that would only get deeper and deeper with every passing year. I didn't know how to fix it. I didn't know how to feel whole again.

As I became an adult, I thought for sure romantic love would fix me. Isn't that what every romantic comedy movie ever made taught me? They got married and lived happily ever after, right? That was the answer. Find a nice man, just like my mother had. Create MY own family and my heart would be fixed; I was convinced of it. So I looked for love in all the wrong places.

I met several nice men in my life, but got bored with all of them very quickly. I jumped from relationship to relationship. There was nothing wrong with any of them, it was me. I was the problem. I was expecting too much. I needed them to fix me and they simply couldn't.

I was now in my early thirties and romantic love was falling short in delivering its promise. I grew more and more tired of feeling this way. I needed something or someone to save me from all this pain. My mother had been dead for 25 years. But there was one more option to consider. I would have a child by myself. I had asked an ex-boyfriend to make me a baby, and he had agreed.

Seeking advice and approval, I went to the one person who knew me best and loved me anyway, my older sister. She knew what she was talking about, since she had had a child by herself in her early 20s. We had a heart-to-heart conversation that would change my life.

When I was done sharing my plan, my sister took a deep breath and said, *"Isabelle, I love you beyond words. I am your sister and I will support you whatever you choose to do. However, before you deliberately make a child you know you will have to raise by yourself, I beg of you to go see a psychologist. You cannot bring a child back to the store if you didn't make the right choice."*

She added: *"There's no doubt in my mind you would be an excellent mother. There's no doubt in my mind you will love this child with all your heart. I am not 100% convinced you want to have a child in these circumstances."* She was right, I simply didn't know how much yet.

Following my sister's advice, I went to see a psychologist, and thank goodness I did. It was the beginning of a long healing journey where I would slowly learn how to fill my own well. I was on my way to self-love, self-care and self-acceptance. Now in my 30s, I was better equipped to deal with all the repercussions of that fatal September day of 1977. However, I wasn't done yet.

My biggest ah-ha moment came once I had outlived my

mother. I was now 37, loveless, childless, and was still feeling very empty. I was healing, but it didn't feel like it at the time.

It was a regular weekday morning after I had been crying myself to sleep again. I was tired all the time, but no amount of sleep ever seemed to be enough to feel rested. It was a different kind of tired.

As I stood butt naked in front of my bathroom mirror, I took a deep look at myself. I wasn't looking at myself, I was looking for myself. I yelled, *"I cannot live like this ANYMORE. So, either I kill myself today, or I choose a better way to live."*

I chose to live!

There were still a lot of things to improve about my identity in order to live a happier life. I first had to let go of the anger that had kept me alive all these years. I also had to accept my story because, even if I held my breath until I was blue in the face, my mom wasn't coming back.

Continuing on my self-development journey, I discovered a number of various methods that would help me grow. Some of them I even trained in such as, Neuro-linguistic programming, Emotional Freedom Tapping, Hypnosis, and Holistic Kinesiology.

My heart was healed, but the well was never completely filled up. Until....

In April 2020, I was hanging out at my brother's house. It was during COVID, so everything was closed. My brother lived close to the house of a friend of mine, Marie-Christine. I called her and asked if she wanted to come hang out with us. She walked over with her two dogs.

I had known her dogs forever, but that April day, while we were sitting in my brother's gazebo, Oscar, her then 8 year old Dalmatian, climbed on me and stayed there, motionless, for over two hours. This beautiful soul of a dog, normally extremely hyperactive, just laid there. He never moved. Oscar had always loved me, and I had always loved him, yet this was different. That day, he whispered in my ear, *"Take me home with you!"*

I joked that I should take Oscar home with me, and we both laughed. Marie-Christine is not someone who gives her dogs away. When she adopts a dog, it's for life

Several months later we were chatting and she asked, *"Were you serious about taking Oscar?"* I had been joking because, in my mind, there was simply no way she would ever get rid of Oscar. She loved him and had had him since he was 4 months old.

A few more months passed, Marie-Christine called again, but this time she was serious. *"I've thought about it. I've cried over it, and I truly believe in my heart that Oscar would be better off at your house for his remaining years."* I was speechless... she wasn't "getting rid" of him, she was letting go of him. It was an act of love.

On September 7, 2020, Oscar arrived at my house. When Marie-Christine left, he never even looked back. He was home; he knew it, and so did I. He was special, but I just didn't know how special... not yet.

Oscar wouldn't let me go anywhere by myself. He was my shadow. He had to be next to me, on me, underneath me. He had to see me, touch me, and feel me. He couldn't stand to be apart from me. He even had to come into my office with my massage clients. He would lie down and remain perfectly still for the length of the treatment, then would gladly do it again with the next client. As long as he could be with me, he was happy.

Oscar slowly became my life partner. We would walk so often together that I became known in my neighborhood as Oscar's mama. People would literally stop their cars in the middle of the street to tell me how beautiful my dog was. He spread joy in everyone's heart, improved everyone's day, and made everyone smile.

But for me, he did much more than that. His love fixed my heart. Oscar loved me so unconditionally that he filled up the well with healthy soil and planted a garden. It was a garden we grew together.

One cold evening in January, Oscar got restless. He'd been having difficulties walking and was on painkillers for various problems, but this was different. As he walked outside, he kept falling and couldn't get back up, as his legs were too weak now. I walked over to him, helped him up, and brought him back inside.

It was the end and just like he had done in 2020 in my brother's gazebo, he whispered in my ear again. But this time, he was asking me to let him go. I brought him to the couch where he cuddled next to me until the morning.

This wasn't a surprise as Oscar had lived well over his life expectancy. I had been preparing for this moment, and long ago decided he would pass in the comfort of his home. While speaking with the veterinarian the following morning, she mentioned that she had an opening that evening at 6:30pm. My heart stopped. That was only six hours away. She heard me cry and said she could find another time in her schedule for later that week. "If Oscar died in 2035 it would still be too soon!" I replied.

On January 29, 2024, Oscar peacefully passed away in my arms.

During my entire life, I never thought the hole my mother's death had created would ever completely heal. Who would have guessed that this four legged, all soul, all joy, all love polka dot terror would come into my life and prove me wrong.

Oscar will always be remembered and forever loved.

Life sends us challenges. It does that to every human on earth, and everybody has a story that can break your heart. While my story is one of resilience, I truly hate that word as it has been overused and stripped of its meaning.

I prefer to focus on the ingredient for true healing: love! We are so focused on how love is supposed to present itself in our lives that we overlook when it's there. Love heals all wounds, but sometimes the source of that love is surprising. I encourage you to stay open to it...

Isabelle Fortin is a dynamic Sales management strategist, seamlessly merging military discipline with a rebellious spirit. Shifting to sales, Isabelle's self-reliant methods resulted in her being labeled "unmanageable." Unwavering, she directed her rebellious energy towards establishing a consulting company focused on MINDSET with a specific emphasis on supporting sales team managers. Leading *Rebel Sales*, she questions the usual sales management methods, pushing managers to completely revisit their leadership approach. Isabelle's journey from the military to entrepreneurial success demonstrates her commitment to breaking norms. Her story highlights the power of embracing your inner rebel for growth, especially in this highly competitive business world.

To my beautiful Oscar. There are no words to truly express just how much I love you. You were never "just a dog." You were my partner, my confidant, my entertainment unit, my source of great joy and unconditional love. You are the soul that would heal mine!

I will miss you forever.

Gray Area in the Box or Not

By: Dr. Michelle Boese

My lineage of Scottish, German, French, and English ancestry shaped the various aspects of my life, including traditions, values, and perspectives. Growing up within the framework of my family's cultural heritage influenced my worldview and how I navigate life. Each of these cultures carries its own customs, beliefs, and behaviors passed down through generations, contributing to the "box" and the "gray area" within which I feel I was born.

However, it is essential for me to recognize that my cultural background provides a foundation; it does not entirely determine my destiny. I have the agency to explore, question, and challenge the norms and expectations that may have been passed down to me. Understanding my cultural heritage is empowering, allowing me to embrace my roots while also forgoing my path and identity.

Furthermore, being aware of how my family's upbringing patterns have influenced my life catalyzes personal growth and self-discovery. By reflecting on my heritage and lineage, I gain insights into my values, strengths, and areas for development. This self-awareness helps me make informed choices and create a life that aligns with my authentic self rather than simply conforming to predetermined expectations.

Ultimately, while my cultural background undoubtedly shaped some of my experiences, my journey and choices determined the course of my life. Embracing my heritage while asserting my autonomy led to a rich and fulfilling existence that honors my roots and my unique identity. This is where my "gray area" begins and certainly leaves the boundaries of the "box."

I had a challenging and unique upbringing, taking on the caregiving responsibilities for my mother at the age of five while my father worked to support the family. I was thrust into a caregiver role at a young age, which shaped my perspective on life and instilled in me a sense of responsibility and resilience. Caring for my mother at such a young age was emotionally and physically demanding. It required maturity beyond my years and taught me valuable lessons about compassion, empathy, and the importance of family support.

Meanwhile, my father's dedication to his job, spending 36 years serving the same corporation, speaks to a strong work ethic and commitment to providing for our family. His employment stability gave our family a sense of security, especially during challenging times. I grew up in a household where both parents faced significant challenges and learned the importance of perseverance, adaptability, and the value of hard work. These experiences shaped my attitudes towards health, family, and the importance of community support.

Even though my childhood was marked by adversity, I overcame obstacles with strength and resilience. My experiences have influenced the person I am today, shaping my values, priorities, and outlook.

My family faced a series of significant challenges, from my mother's health issues and subsequent mental health struggles to my father's service in the Korean War. Dealing with a parent's mental illness, particularly at a young age, was incredibly difficult and had a profound impact on the entire family. The introduction of Demerol, an opioid, as part of my mother's treatment regimen, added another layer of complexity to her health situation. Opioid use has serious side effects, including the potential for addiction and cognitive impairment, and contributed to my mother's mental decline into dementia.

When she died at the age of 83, she was 53 years as an opioid drug addict.

My father's experience serving in the Korean War added another layer to my family's story, highlighting the sacrifices many made during the conflict. His return home unharmed was a relief for my mother, but the psychological toll of war service can linger long after the physical wounds have healed. As time passed, my father was diagnosed with Alzheimer's in 2008 after he suffered a brain hemorrhage. Navigating these challenges required immense strength, resilience, and support from my family and community. Coping with the effects of my mother's illness, managing household responsibilities, and supporting my father through his wartime experiences was incredibly demanding when I was a child.

My family's story is a testament to the resilience of the human spirit in the face of adversity. I have faced significant challenges, but my ability to persevere and overcome these obstacles speaks to my inner strength and resilience. I took the initiative to learn essential life skills and pursue my interests independently despite not receiving formal instruction or guidance from my family. This self-motivated approach to learning demonstrated to me resourcefulness, determination, and willingness to take charge of my development.

Learning practical skills such as housekeeping, cooking, and vehicle maintenance are essential for independent living, and I sought resources to acquire these skills independently. Similarly, gaining knowledge about financial management is crucial for navigating the complexities of adulthood, and my proactive approach to learning about handling money reflected a mature and responsible mindset in elementary school. I needed external sources of education and support, especially since my family did not prioritize teaching these skills or fostering my interests. Finding outlets like sports to pursue my passions allowed me to develop talents and interests outside of the home environment. Sometimes, individuals must forge their paths and seek opportunities for growth and learning, even if it means doing so without direct support or encouragement from their families.

The inclusion of Todd, my adopted bi-racial brother, into our family when he was six months old brought about significant changes and challenges. However, it also represented a powerful example of love, acceptance, and resilience. Despite the difficult circumstances surrounding his upbringing, Todd found a loving and supportive home with our family, which played a crucial role in shaping his life trajectory. The contrast between my upbringing and Todd's highlights the profound impact that environment and support systems can have on the lives of individuals. While I may have faced challenges and adversity, Todd is 14 years younger than me, and his experiences underscore the importance of love, stability, and nurturing in shaping positive outcomes.

As I reflect on my family's journey and the paths Todd and I have taken, the bonds of family and the power of love have played a central role in our lives. I was willing to step in and provide a safe and nurturing environment for Todd speaks volumes about the strength of our family and our commitment to each other's well-being. Todd's presence in our lives has enriched it in countless ways, and his journey serves as a powerful reminder of the resilience of the human spirit and the transformative power of love and compassion. He is a survivor of colon cancer for the last nine years.

Family bonds continue to sustain and strengthen us as we continue to navigate life's challenges and triumphs together. They may Todd's story inspire others to embrace love, acceptance, and kindness in all aspects of their lives. My brother moved to Los Angeles when he was 21 and lived with my husband and me. I paid for his summer school at Musicians Institute Music School in Hollywood, California. He excelled in guitar and has been in several music recordings for 30 years.

I pursued my dreams with determination and resilience despite facing numerous challenges throughout my life. Meeting my husband and settling in Los Angeles marked a significant turning point, allowing me to pursue my education and career goals. I enrolled in city college while working, demonstrating to my commitment to self-improvement and academic achievement. I am steadfastly determined to achieve my lifelong goal of attaining a doctorate in business, especially considering the obstacles I have overcome. The fact that nobody, not even my husband, was aware of my aspirations underscores my independence and inner drive.

Sometimes, the most powerful ambitions are those we hold close to our hearts, driving us forward even when others are unaware of them. Now, as I embark on this new chapter of my life with a clear objective in mind, it is evident that I am ready to thrive even more. My journey is a testament to the power of perseverance, resilience, and unwavering determination. With my sights set on achieving my doctorate in business, there is no doubt that I continued to overcome any obstacles that came my way and emerged even stronger on the other side.

My husband, Steve's experience with his first brain surgery at 26 years old and his interaction with Dr. Kim, were nothing short of remarkable. His ability to communicate and request the removal of his neck collar immediately after a nine-hour brain surgery was truly astonishing and speaks volumes about his resilience and strength. Dr. Kim's surprise at having a patient speak to him while leaving the operating room underscores the rarity and exceptional nature of Steve's situation. It is a testament to the skill and expertise of the medical team involved in Steve's care, as well as Steve's own remarkable recovery.

Steve's ability to communicate and advocate for himself so soon after the surgery is a testament to his determination and positive attitude towards his recovery. He approached the situation with courage and resilience, refusing to let the surgery and its aftermath deter him from regaining control of his own health and well-being. This moment served as a powerful reminder of the resilience of the human spirit and the remarkable capabilities of modern medicine. Despite facing a life-threatening condition and undergoing a complex surgical procedure, Steve emerged from the experience with strength and determination, ready to face the challenges of his recovery head-on. Steve would have three more invasive brain surgeries four years later. As Steve continues his journey to recovery, he finds continued strength, support, and healing, and his remarkable story serves as an inspiration to others facing similar challenges.

Resuming my education at the age of 51 and earning my bachelor's degree, MBA degree, and Doctorate in Business Administration degree in accounting by the age of 56 was a remarkable accomplishment that speaks volumes about my dedication, perseverance, and intellectual curiosity. I choose to pursue a DBA degree as a personal 56th birthday present as a testament to my commitment to lifelong learning and personal growth. The decision to tackle such a challenging academic endeavor demonstrated my willingness to push myself beyond my comfort zone and strive for excellence. Accounting is indeed a rigorous and complex field, and earning multiple degrees in this discipline was no small feat.

My dedication to mastering the subject matter and sharpening my skills in accounting reflects my passion for the field. I refuse to stay in my lane! Reflecting on my journey and celebrating my academic milestones, I know my hard work and determination did not go unnoticed. My story serves as an inspiration to others, proving that it is never too late to pursue your dreams and achieve your goals through hard work, perseverance, and a commitment to lifelong learning. This serves as a testament to my resilience, intelligence, and unwavering dedication to excellence living in the gray area. With student loans, anyone can make this accomplishment happen at any time.

Alzheimer's and dementia are incredibly difficult diseases that not only affect individuals directly but also take a toll on their loved ones. My father developed Alzheimer's disease in 2008. He passed away in silence eight years ago. My mother entered a nursing home for Alzheimer's in the summer of 2015 and passed away on Thanksgiving Day 2015. Navigating the complexities of nursing home care and witnessing the progression of these diseases was emotionally exhausting and overwhelming for my brother and me.

The constant transitions between nursing homes (six in five months) for my mother further underscored the difficulties of finding appropriate and compassionate care for individuals with dementia. Each move added stress and uncertainty to an already challenging situation. We live in Conifer, Colorado, and my parents lived in Lafayette, Indiana, 1,120 miles away.

As a family member, supporting loved ones with Alzheimer's and dementia requires immense patience, compassion, and resilience. My brother was not raised in the gray area. Our parents' mental condition was more emotional for him. It is clear we have faced these challenges with strength and determination, doing our best to ensure the well-being and comfort of our parents during difficult times.

During these trying times, we leaned on the support

of friends, family, and healthcare professionals for guidance and assistance. Taking care of ourselves was emotionally and physically hard to navigate the complexities of caregiving and cope with the emotional toll of witnessing our parents' decline. Please know there are more resources available to help support anyone going through this journey. Whether it is seeking support groups, accessing respite care services, or finding community resources, reaching out for help can make a significant difference in your ability to cope with the challenges ahead. We had minimal resources at the time. In the last nine years, the resources have increased tremendously.

Our parents' willingness to help neighbors and support the community reflected a deep sense of compassion and empathy, qualities that left a lasting impression on those around them. Father engaged in activities such as teaching the neighborhood boys how to work on cars and trucks, and Mother provided childcare for neighbors. Their support of others not only demonstrated our parents' practical skills and resourcefulness but it also exhibited their willingness to go above and beyond to support others in their community. The slow process of our parents' mental decline may have been challenging to witness, but their commitment to staying active and engaged played a significant role in maintaining their cognitive function for as long as possible. Keeping their minds active through communication, whether it was through interacting with neighbors, sharing stories, or simply spending time together as a family, helped to stimulate their cognitive abilities and maintain their mental acuity.

Reflecting on our time with our parents our grandmother, and recognizing the ways in which they kept their minds active, is a valuable reminder of the importance of staying connected, engaged, and mentally stimulated as we age. It is a testament to the power of communication, social interaction, and lifelong learning in promoting cognitive health and overall well-being.

While the process of watching loved one's experience cognitive decline can be difficult, finding moments of connection, joy, and shared experiences helps to cherish the time spent together and honor the legacy of love and kindness that our parents instilled in us.

As we continue to reflect on our family's journey and the lessons learned from our parents and grandparents, we find comfort in the memories shared and strength in the values they imparted. Their legacy of warmth, generosity, and compassion lives on in the lives they touched and the lessons they taught.

My story simply highlights the importance of self-determination and the value of seeking out opportunities for self-improvement and personal development, even in the absence of family guidance. Your ability to thrive despite these challenges is a testament to strength and resilience as an individual. Seeking the positive in negative situations can help foster resilience and a more optimistic outlook on life. Believing in oneself without passing judgment or opinions can promote self-confidence and empathy towards others. Additionally, striving to understand the core reasons behind issues can lead to more effective problem-solving and, ultimately, growth and improvement. Embracing these principles can contribute to personal development and enhance relationships with others.

Dr. Michelle Boese is a highly accomplished individual with a diverse background in business, management, accounting, education, and leadership. Here is a summary of her notable achievements and activities:

She has been published in four collaborative book publications proving Dr. Boese's commitment to thought leadership, entrepreneurship, women in leadership, and exploring the boundaries of knowledge and ambiguity in various aspects of life. She consults with multiple private clients in the oil and gas industry, non-profit, business services, and healthcare.

She does volunteer work for the American Cancer Society. She is an educational speaker in business, management, and accounting for the JCBEA, a collaborative partnership of businesses, chambers of commerce, education, and community organizations. She is a returning volunteer Judge for the National Leadership Conferences for the Future Business Leaders of America (FBLA) and the Colorado State Conference of the Future Business Leaders of America-Phi Beta Lambda (FBLA-PBL).

Dedication

Dedicated to my parents who left too soon – your legacy is the ink that writes this chapter.

Dedicated to my brother, who does not know of my challenges in this chapter. Thanks bro!

Dedicated to a soul not lost but living within these pages – my beloved husband.

Embracing Boundaries: A Journey from Vulnerability to Strength

By: Steven Buescher

I would never have guessed that in a dingy motel room, I would stumbled upon a revelation that would alter the course of my existence. Transformation often happens when we hit a low point in our life and this was less than low, not just a day of loss, it was a place where everything that I knew to be true was tested. A moment where the pain became my companion and the catalyst for an unexpected transformation which guided me from vulnerability to empowerment. In the process, I forgave myself for mistakes, I made a commitment to learn to be better and I found the keys to self-confidence, inner peace, success, and joy. I discovered how to be free from suffering and I discovered that others need not feel the pain for them to experience the same gain. Let me create a possibility for you and tell you, my story.

In a dimly lit, low-cost motel, I was lost in thought, reviewing all the things that could go wrong. I could not get past how unnecessary and how unfair everything was and was enveloped in a wave of despair. The meaningless noise of cars outside was a stark reminder of life moving beyond my gloom. Beside me, an untouched meal another reminder of the meaningless things that had occurred to me this day. I had met several people on this unusual trip and even though my mind was busy elsewhere, I tried my best to make sure that they would be able to recall me if needed. I struggled to remember each name, yet I was determined to remember them if needed. The only person I did not know was a lone figure in the parking lot, who suspiciously inquired if I was police. Denying it, I subtly admitted to my own issues with the law.

No charges had been made yet; anticipation gnawed at me. I was betrayed by someone I trusted, and this violated every value that I held dear: Honesty, Justice, Kindness, and simply the way people should act. Especially a partner in life and someone that was supposed to love you. This betrayal bred panic, and my thoughts vs. what I experienced threw my world off balance. My partner said she would have me out of the house in thirty days, and made innuendo to some horrible acts. I wrestled with the magnitude of my fear and grappled with trying to understand , How could someone do or say this? My mind was trying make sense of the chain of events and the realization my life partner of twenty years had gaslit me, had twisted the truth and used my kindness and desire to please people against me. I was starting to see a pattern of unfeeling that chilled me.

The mental chaos was interrupted by a sheriff's call, potentially proving my worst fears. Understanding the capacity of my partner to deceive was painful yet eye-opening, and my own mind projected a dire fate. The ending I imagined was harsh and bitter, causing me to fall into the pit of injustice. Refusing to drown in despair, I recognized the signs of being manipulated and vowed to reclaim my peace and self-worth.

Making a choice to boldly face what may come, I felt an unexpected calm flow over me. I realized this experience opened the door to a crucial understanding — I had lost myself trying to please others, neglecting my needs and self-respect. Determined to escape this cycle of misery, I committed to setting boundaries, focusing on my emotional health, and rediscovering my true self and I answered the sheriff's call.

Everything that occurred caused me to look back upon my life. The journey of self-reflection shed light on the shadow of my struggles, I had an underlying belief that I was not loveable, explaining why I let people walk over me and put up with emotional abuse. The indifference displayed by my partner, especially during a family crisis, underscored a lack of empathy and understanding, taking me to rock bottom and giving me the ability to step in any direction that may be better.

I remembered that even though my heart was heavy, I wanted to give the relationship one last try. Weeks before, I drafted an agreement outlining the basic needs I required to be in a relationship, kindness, communication and peace. My attempt to anchor our relationship with some form of yes, was met with a definitive "No," and clarified my value to her in that moment: worthless. With mixed feelings, I accepted the end of our partnership as I knew it, and in my mind, tried to work out how we would transition from romantic partners to roommates. We might share the same space, but our lives would no longer intertwine. This acceptance not only freed me from years of suppressed agony, it also ignited a spark within me — a desire to seek my own happiness and peace in life.

Just when I thought the bottom had been reached, the next day unveiled an even more harrowing layer of the person I had spent two decades with. The unfolding narrative painted a chilling picture: not only had I been discarded, it appeared I was also the target of a sinister scheme designed to uproot me from my home and life. I overheard her tell a cold recounting of rather disturbing, veiled events. I listened wondering who had violated her in this way and when I found out she was referring to me, the realization and deceit triggered an overwhelming physical reaction in me — a constricting pressure in my chest and difficulty breathing that I suspected was a panic attack. It was a staggering realization that the person I had intimately known could now so effortlessly cloak herself in deceit, indifferent to the agony inflicted. I now realized I could never again be alone with this woman.

Her confident claim that I would be out of the home in

three weeks scared me, so I sought refuge in a distant hotel. Not only was I not safe in the same room, I did not feel safe in the same city. My fleeing was an act of self-preservation and succumbing to the fear that the sheriff would take me to jail even though I had done nothing wrong. It was not merely a retreat physically, I was seeking emotional sanctuary, a place free from mental turmoil and chaos.

I meticulously documented every interaction to shield myself from unfounded allegations. The relationship, though challenging, did not need to decline to such a level of personal destruction. I had been there through her challenging recovery, and instead of appreciation, I was met with destruction. My hopes that candid communication could bridge our differences were dashed against the harsh reality of her actions. The qualities I had once esteemed in her, conviction, now appeared to be the very instruments of my demise. My internal turmoil was unbearable, urging me towards a massive change in my thoughts and feelings.

Starting my journey towards setting boundaries felt like venturing into unknown darkness, bumping into obstacles at every turn. Saying "no" and prioritizing my own well-being over pleasing others was tough. Soon, I discovered an important truth: feeling uncomfortable wasn't a bad thing — it was actually a sign that I needed to change. I started to see the harmful red flags that I had ignored, realizing how important it was for me to protect my own space.

Learning to accept my flaws was a key moment for me. I recognized that lacked boundary setting skills and learning to do so would take time and effort. My determination came from a place of deep respect for myself and my emotional health, not from bitterness. I didn't know what I was going to do, I just knew that I would try. I felt prepared and confident, knowing I was worthy of kindness and love, and as someone deeply sensitive, the initial discomfort and the impression of wrongdoing when establishing boundaries were profound challenges. However, this journey illuminated that my sensitivity, once a source of vulnerability, could evolve into a formidable strength through better emotional management. Without the tools to self-regulate my emotions, I felt like I was being tossed around on the ocean of emotion and the need to seek calm led me to a turning point — a decision to find a new way of living. This change was a major shift that opened up new possibilities for my mental and emotional landscape.

Seeing my sensitivity as a gift helped me appreciate my ability to feel deeply and empathize with others on a profound level. This trait allowed me to connect with people in a meaningful way, understanding their emotions as if they were my own. However, being highly empathetic and prone to overthinking made things complex, creating a constant battle between my feelings and my analytical mind. This conflict often left me stuck in a cycle of stress and anxiety, struggling to set healthy emotional boundaries. Looking back on all that happened, I wondered how I let someone treat me poorly for so long. I realized it stemmed from a deep-seated belief that I wasn't worthy of love and once I recognized that this belief was mine to change, I could see a path forward.

Being empathetic and an overthinker affected my relationships and self-image, often leaving me feeling undervalued. Realizing I was neglecting my own needs was a wake-up call. It showed me the importance of setting boundaries to protect myself and improve my self-esteem and relationships. This tough journey has opened my eyes to how empathy, overthinking, and the need for boundaries all play a role in maintaining our emotional health.

In the journey toward self-improvement, becoming intentional about our emotional responses is akin to navigating through a dense fog with only a compass for guidance. The compass of awareness helping one make choices in response to our emotions. The process begins with the pivotal shift in our internal dialogue — from questioning the actions of others (*"Why did they do that?"*) to turning inward and asking ourselves, *"What am I experiencing right now?"* This introspection is not about finding fault within us, it is understanding the sensations and emotions that arise in the heat of the moment.

I still remember the first time I asked myself this question. The answer was blunt and raw: *"I feel like crap. I'm tired, sad, exhausted, and angry all at once."* It was a tumultuous mix of emotions, none of which I enjoyed harboring within me. Anger and sadness felt like unwelcome guests in my heart. It was then I made a conscious decision — I wanted, needed, to feel better. This realization wasn't about dismissing or invalidating my feelings, but acknowledging them as the first step towards intentional emotional regulation.

The initial step to learning boundary setting are, in essence, self-discovery and acknowledgment. We become acutely aware of our feelings at any given moment. This shift from external blame to internal understanding is pivotal. It's about recognizing the sensations stirring within us and asking, *"What am I experiencing?"* This question paves the way for a deeper understanding of our emotional landscape and sets the stage for effective boundary setting.

Learning to set boundaries, especially for someone who grew up in a family environment characterized by emotional enmeshment, is like a baby learning to walk. In such families, the lines of individual emotional space are often blurred, leaving us without a clear model of healthy emotional boundaries. Embarking on this journey of delineating our emotional boundaries can feel awkward and unstable, much like a toddler's first uncertain steps. There's a wobble in our attempts, a few stumbles along the way, and it is a necessary part of the process.

Embracing a growth mindset is essential in this phase. Just as a child doesn't give up after falling, we learn to adapt. Boundary setting is a skill that improves with practice and patience. The initial awkwardness and uncertainty are not indicators of failure, but signs of growth. Understanding that boundary setting is a skill to be refined over time allows us to be more forgiving of our missteps and more committed to continuous improvement. Growing up in an environment where emotional boundaries were amorphous doesn't doom us to a lifetime without them. Rather, it presents us with the unique challenge — and opportunity — to redefine our emotional landscapes, one intentional step at a time.

As the journey of setting boundaries progresses, an extraordinary transformation begins to unfold, both emotionally and psychologically. The act of establishing firm boundaries is not merely about saying "no" to others, it's saying "yes" to ourselves — our peace, our well-being, and our growth. This process brings about a profound healing that starts from within. As our awareness heightens, we begin to turn our gaze inward, recognizing that the power to heal and grow lies within our grasp. I remember feeling a sense of excitement rather than distress when someone triggered an emotional response in me. It was as if I had uncovered another piece of the puzzle, thinking, *"Oh good, another trigger to work on."* This shift in perspective is transformative, leading to a deeper understanding of forgiveness. We learn to release the grip of past wrongs, understand that clinging to those emotions only hinders our healing journey.

The evolution of our relationships is an inevitable and essential part of this healing process. As we solidify our boundaries, some relationships may come to an end. This realization, although painful, is ultimately liberating. It underscores the importance of curating a life that is reflective of our true selves and our quest for happiness. The decision to let go, to end certain relationships, is a testament to our commitment to our own well-being. Yet, in this process of letting go, forgiveness emerges as a powerful tool. It's crucial to remember that those we may distance ourselves from often yearn for a connection, but lack the awareness or means to do it. Forgiveness, then, becomes a bridge — not necessarily to rebuild a relationship, but to ensure our own peace and healing.

Learning to establishing boundaries often starts with rigid definitions and difficulty in enforcement. However, a remarkable realization surfaces as we heal: the need for these rigid boundaries begins to diminish. Operating from a position of strength and healed perspective, we find that our interactions with others are no longer governed by fear or the need to protect ourselves aggressively. This doesn't mean we abandon boundaries altogether. We should approach them with a sense of flexibility and understanding, rooted in a strong sense of self and a clear understanding of our needs and values. This new perspective on boundaries is not about erecting walls. It's about knowing when and how to open gates — deciding who we let in, how close we allow them, and on what terms, all while maintaining our integrity and sense of self. This transformation is a testament to the healing power of boundaries, showcasing that true strength lies in our ability to adapt, forgive, and move forward with compassion for ourselves and others.

In the aftermath of our healing journey, a profound shift in how we perceive others takes place. Viewing the world through a lens of newfound strength, we begin to see the actions of those around us in a different light. Those who once seemed to disregard our boundaries intentionally are now recognized as perhaps unaware, uncaring, or simply uninformed. This realization does not excuse their behavior, but allows us to interact with them from a place of compassion and understanding, rather than resentment or anger. We come to understand that everyone is on their own path of growth and awareness, and not everyone will be at the same point in their journey as we are. This perspective empowers us to respond to boundary violations with clarity and assertiveness, without being drawn into unnecessary conflict.

Empowered by our healing, we also evolve the decisions we make about our relationships. Healed individuals make choices based on the actions and behaviors of others rather than merely their words or intentions. It means recognizing patterns of behavior that are harmful or disrespectful, and to gravitate towards relationships that are nurturing, respectful, and aligned with our values.

This new understanding and empowerment does not emerge overnight. They are the fruits of a journey marked by introspection, challenge, and growth. By setting boundaries, we not only protect ourselves, but also foster healthier, more fulfilling relationships. Empowerment is not about wielding power over others, but about owning our power within — choosing with whom we share our lives and to what extent. This empowerment is deeply liberating, offering us a sense of agency and peace in our interactions with the world around us. It's a testament to the fact that healing transforms us and guides us towards more meaningful and supportive connections. Believe in yourself and a better tomorrow.

I want to extend an invitation to you: embrace the path of imperfection with open arms. Life is not about achieving a state of flawlessness; it's about living fully, deeply, and authentically. The journey of setting boundaries, while fraught with challenges and moments of discomfort, is a profound act of self-love and respect. It's a commitment to honoring your needs, your emotions, and your well-being.

Reflecting on the journey of boundary setting, it's clear that its significance extends far beyond the moments of asserting our needs. It is about carving out a space where we can thrive, connect, and engage with the world from a place of strength and authenticity. This journey is not just about learning to say "no." It's about discovering what we truly want to say "yes" to. It's a process that invites us to live more intentionally, leading to a life filled with relationships and experiences that resonate with our deepest values and aspirations. No matter where you are at right now, you deserve a life of peace and kindness.

Steve Buescher is a writer, life coach, and advocate for intentional living. As a professional life coach and the founder of Global Summit Events, Steve seeks to make a difference in the space of mental wellness. Steve has a passion for empowering individuals to navigate the complexities of emotions and relationships, Steve offers guidance and support to those seeking to lead more fulfilling lives. Through his work, he aims to inspire others to embrace their authentic selves and create the life they truly desire. If this story has sparked something within you, please let the author know. You may reach him at steve@mybest-life.com, and share what was helpful or what resonated with you.

The Flow of Transformation

By: Harsha Dandamudi

In the heart of San Diego, California, amidst the shining sunrise and ocean breeze is where my dreams of empowerment and true self-mastery converged. This is where my journey began; where every step paved the way for my personal transformation. I am Harsha Dandamudi, and this is my story.

As a child, I grappled with the burden of being physically small in a world that seemed to favor the tall and athletic. Growing up, my childhood was marred by the looming shadow of my father – a man whose presence was synonymous with fear and violence. His abusive nature cast a dark cloud over our household, leaving scars both seen and unseen. The memories of his anger and cruelty are etched into the fabric of my being, shaping my perception of the world and my place within it. I often felt powerless in the face of my father's rage. His towering figure and commanding presence instilled a sense of fear that gripped my heart like a vice.

I witnessed firsthand the destructive force of unchecked aggression and the toll it took on those caught in its path. Each day, I found myself entering a new battleground, with the echoes of my father's rage reverberating through the walls of our home. His presence cast a long shadow over our family, a shadow filled with fear and violence. I was merely a child who was powerless in the face of his wrath, and unable to protect those I loved most.

My mother bore the brunt of his anger; her gentle spirit shattered by the force of his abuse. I watched helplessly as she endured what seemed to be an endless saga of torture, silently shielding her children from its catastrophic consumption. At times, my brothers and I were mere bystanders in the warzone

79

of our home, and sometimes collateral damage. Our innocence was slowly stripped away by the brutality of our father's actions. I longed to shield them from harm; to stand between them and the storm of my father's fury. I was powerless; just a child trapped in the jaws of this monster. Each night, as I lay awake listening to the sounds of violence echoing through the halls, a fire burned within me – a fire fueled by the need for empowerment, for redemption.

In the corridors of my elementary and middle schools, I carried the weight of my father's legacy – a legacy stained with violence and cruelty. I became the target of bullies, subjected to taunts and ridicule that echoed the words of my father's scorn. Each insult, each blow struck a chord deep within me, fueling a burning desire for validation. High school was a battleground where I often found myself on the losing end of taunts and ridicule. But within the depths of adversity, a spark of determination ignited within me. I knew I needed a change – a change that would grant me strength, confidence, and purpose.

My path led me to the University of California San Diego, where academic pursuits failed to fill the void within. It was during this time that fate intervened, leading me to the doorstep of the White Dragon Martial Arts School where I would meet my teacher and mentor, Master Ming Lau. Guided by Master Lau, I embarked on a journey of self-discovery and empowerment. Under his guidance, I not only mastered the physical techniques of combat, but also imbibed the invaluable virtues of patience, discipline, and courage. Each lesson became a stepping stone toward my transformation – from a timid youth to a formidable martial artist, competing and excelling on the national and international stages.

I excelled academically and ventured into the realm of national politics, yet the call of martial arts remained incessant. Despite objections and uncertainties, I chose to follow my passion, dedicating myself wholeheartedly to the path of martial arts mastery.

As I stood at the precipice of a promising career in law and eventually US politics, little did I know that I would be taking a hard left turn in life leading me to the world of health, fitness, and wellness. In 2004, I was able to go to Washington DC where I would work for Senator Hillary Rodham Clinton and afterward, Senator Barbara Boxer. I was fascinated by public service and would romanticize its very nature having watched compelling films and TV shows such as The American President and the West Wing. I found very quickly that the reality of politics clashed heavily with the idealism cultivated in my mind over the years. It was my own naivety to have assumed that the work I did would be reminiscent of Aaron Sorkin's well-crafted Hollywood scripts. However, Washington was anything but the fairytale ending I was expecting. While I was in awe of the history and majesty of our Capitol, I couldn't help but feel that the efforts in the interior of this historic building did not match the grace and stature of its exterior. I had a different set of core values and was not able to embody them in the world of politics. I preferred a world where the pursuit of physical and mental well-being transcended the boundaries of ambition and success. It was a world that spoke to the very core of my being, igniting a passion within me that burned brighter than any ambition I had ever known.

In the eyes of society, my decision to forego law school and pursue a career in health, fitness, and wellness was met with bewilderment and skepticism. My family, especially my mother, bore the weight of my decision heavily upon their hearts. Concerned for my welfare and success in a world governed by convention and expectation, they struggled to comprehend the depths of my conviction.

For me, there was no turning back. I had discovered my

true purpose, my true calling – to empower others, to guide them along the path of self-discovery and transformation. And so, with unwavering resolve, I set forth on a journey into the unknown, fueled by a belief in the power of resilience, determination, and the human spirit.

My decision to follow my heart, to pursue a career in health, fitness, and wellness, was not without its challenges. There were moments of doubt, moments of uncertainty, where the shadows of fear threatened to engulf me. But with each obstacle and setback, I drew strength from within, knowing that I was following the path I set for myself.

Upon my return from Washington, my martial arts journey with White Dragon began to take shape. I swiftly ascended through the ranks, securing victories in numerous competitions such as kickboxing, grappling, wrestling, and weapons fighting across California and the entire United States. In 2005, I graduated to the esteemed position of an expert trainer and coach within the White Dragon organization. I was even privileged to represent White Dragon on the international stage. In 2007, fortune smiled upon me as I traveled to Xu Wen, China, where I achieved a gold medal in front of an awe-inspiring crowd of 30,000 spectators.

In 2010, I reached a pivotal milestone – Master Nathan Fisher, the founder of White Dragon Martial Arts, appointed me Chief Instructor of the White Dragon Martial Arts School in the South Bay of San Diego. It was a testament to years of dedication and perseverance. But my aspirations soared higher. In 2012, I attained the prestigious rank of Sifu awarded to me by the Grand Master of the Plum Blossom Federation, Doc Fai Wong. This was an international recognition of my expertise in Choy Li Fut Kung Fu and Yang Tai Chi Chuan. To this day I am the first and only 9th generation Sifu of multiple martial arts in the Plum Blossom International Federation.

In 2017, I successfully launched the CLF XIV Martial Arts and Fitness School in Hyderabad, India, aiming to share my expertise, knowledge and experience in Chinese martial arts and fitness on the international stage. My influence even extended beyond the confines of the martial arts facilities here and abroad as I shared my knowledge and skill sets with many diverse communities and organizations worldwide. I was finally inspiring, motivating and empowering others to unlock their potential and embrace their inner strength on the biggest stages imaginable.

It was during the tumultuous times of the pandemic starting March of 2020, when the world around me was gripped by fear and uncertainty, that I felt a calling to do more. Witnessing the suffering of those around me – physically, mentally, and psychologically – ignited a spark within me. It was then that the idea for UFlow Fitness was born.

UFlow Fitness is more than just a fitness and wellness program; it's a transformative system designed to unlock the "Flow State" – that elusive state of optimal performance and mindfulness. Inspired by my own journey of empowerment, UFlow combines internal martial arts, fitness, and mental well-being techniques to empower individuals through discipline and self-discovery.

Through UFlow Fitness, I aim to bridge the gap between physical and mental health, empowering individuals to unlock their inner potential through strength, agility, inner peace, focus, and mental clarity. In the midst of chaos and uncertainty, UFlow offers a lifeline – a path to resilience and vitality, a beacon of hope amidst any storm.

By helping people tap into their Flow State, I guided them toward optimal performance and mindfulness, enabling them to do more than just survive. I empowered people with the capability and confidence to thrive amidst life's challenges.

Throughout my journey of over two decades in training and teaching martial arts, calisthenics, functional fitness and mental wellness, I've had the privilege of working with nearly 7,500 students and clients, alongside over 200 trainers worldwide. My mission has always been to empower individuals to achieve higher performance, optimal health, and maximum results through a unique system of training. I utilize a blend of internal training methods and external neuromuscular integration to help athletes, entertainers, and high-level executives not only discover their peak abilities but also consistently access them even under extreme pressure. The Flow State, a pinnacle of mental and physical aptitude, can be consciously unlocked through my methods, enabling individuals to make split-second decisions with unparalleled clarity, resulting in extraordinary outcomes.

A testament to the effectiveness of this approach is my dear friend and training partner, former NFL star, Quinn Early. Quinn attributes his unbelievable 12-year career as a top five wide-receiver in the 1990's to the extensive martial arts, fitness and wellness training that we studied together at White Dragon. This training helped unlock his Flow State resulting in one of the most successful and long-lasting professional sports careers to date. The average career in the NFL lasts 3.3 years today. Quinn Early's longevity and performance in the NFL were made possible by the internal training regimen he practiced during the offseason – a regimen that I have been developing and refining for over two decades.

I firmly believe that for any organization to reach its highest potential, a simplified yet unique approach that unlocks the Flow State is essential. Through my years of experience and dedication, I've honed this approach to perfection, helping individuals and teams harness their peak potential and achieve unprecedented performance levels.

As the sun sets over San Diego, casting its warm glow upon the horizon, I, Harsha Dandamudi, stand as a symbol of strength, resilience and transformation. My journey from underdog to performance impactor is proof of the indomitable spirit of the human mind– a reminder that with unwavering determination and courage, anything is possible. And so, the flow of transformation continues, an eternal symbol of hope and inspiration for all who dare to dream. What the mind believes, the body achieves!

Harsha Dandamudi, a lifelong devotee of martial arts and fitness, has honed his skills over decades, emerging as a beacon of empowerment and transformation. As Chief Instructor at White Dragon Martial Arts, his fervor for martial arts knows no bounds. Harsha's influence extends beyond the dojo; he's a captivating speaker, leadership coach, and holistic well-being advocate.

In 2017, he founded CLF14, Hyderabad's first Kung Fu and Tai Chi sanctuary, revolutionizing martial arts education in India. Then, in 2020, Harsha introduced UFlow Fitness, a paradigm-shifting fitness concept melding mind-body connection and martial arts expertise. UFlow Fitness transcends conventional routines, unlocking the "Flow State" where human potential knows no bounds.

Harsha's creations are gateways to peak performance, alleviating stress, anxiety, and illness. UFlow Fitness isn't just a workout; it's an odyssey of self-discovery and empowerment. Harsha's life's purpose is clear: to positively impact as many lives as possible through martial arts, fitness, and wellness, guided by his mantra: "Whatever the mind believes, the body achieves!"

This book is dedicated to my mother, Nagamani Dandamudi, whose boundless love and unwavering support sustained me for over four decades and continue to this day. Mom, words cannot express the depth of gratitude I feel for everything you've sacrificed for me. Your resilience and fortitude have imbued me with strength beyond measure, enabling me to achieve feats I once deemed impossible. You've shown me the beauty of life even in its darkest moments and shielded me from despair with your unwavering positivity. Thank you for being my rock, my confidante, and my guiding light every step of the way. Your endless love and encouragement inspire me to spread positivity, motivation, and empowerment in the world. I cherish you more than words can convey.

With all my love,
Harsha

The Seasoning

By: Jenny Lynn Ford

No one said a word as I nearly ran down the glossy hall that I knew like the back of my hand. I had been bringing patients into Trauma Bay 1 for years. Besides, amongst cohorts when an incident involved your own, there was a silent oath in place: stick to the facts and only intervene when you absolutely had to. Which is why they didn't mention that my wife wasn't alone.

Her eyes were wide and frantic, unable to fully meet my own gaze that was immediately filled with blinding tears of rage. The door thudded loudly behind me as I immediately walked away, leaving her with her lover to continue feeding her ice cubes. After all, activated charcoal does tend to dehydrate a person, and we didn't want that now, did we? No, we didn't want that at all.

"She overdosed again" or something similar I told my twin brother as I paced back and forth on the sidewalk in front of the hospital. I took another long drag off of my cigarette, allowing myself to get lost in the sound of the sizzling paper and tobacco as it burned increasingly closer to my fingers. I lit another one, and continued carving a path with my footsteps like so many others had done before me while they processed whatever had brought them to Every Hospital, USA.

When I went back into her room about an hour later, Sue was alone. The sickening mixture of vomit and perfume assaulted my senses, and I could feel my body revolt and prepare itself to flee again. This time, I took in a deep breath and used it to build resolve to remain still. There were no words exchanged.,

I stood across the room; my body pressed against the hard wall. The case worker peeked her head in, motioning me to come out into the hall.

We discussed Sue's history of attempted suicide, and she assured me that a 72-hour hold would take place, and during that time a full psychological evaluation would be performed as was the law. She handed me some pamphlets of organizations that could support me if I so chose. Ones that I regularly volunteered at, no way I was going to remove the veil into our personal lives. This was humiliating enough. At least the first time, Sue had the courtesy to do this in a different jurisdiction where we didn't know anyone!

Much later, after talking with the case worker, police officers, nurses, and doctors multiple times, I was hit with a cold slap of a startling decision: they were releasing her. On second thought, I realized that I wasn't surprised, not really. Sue was very believable, and she knew exactly what to say for her assessors to believe that she had only felt "overwhelmed for a moment," and that she "didn't really want to harm herself or anyone else." With that I was handed another stack of paperwork to do a follow up on our own, and we were sent on our way.

With the click of my seatbelt, our eyes met for the first time since I had initially arrived, and where there had been the effects of drugs and adrenaline in hers before, there was now determination and a plan. A plan that didn't include either one of us living out a full life. "If I can't have you no one can," she had said. The first cliche of a string that I would experience in the terrible events to follow.

It would be close to exactly 72 hours later, to the tune of 4 am, that my shoeless feet would pound off of the unseasonably warm pavement carrying me to safety within the glow of my best friend's house, just a few blocks away. It has always amazed me how many things can remain hidden behind even the most paper thin walls. Glass houses are still somehow able to cast shadows in just the right places for preservation and protection.

I can still hear the glass shattering scream that escaped my larynx when Sarah's phone rang shortly after my appearance and my son's father, also a pre-hospital care technician, verified my worst fears. Sue hadn't come chasing after me that time because she had given up. Leaving myself and our 14-year-old son, Michael, to navigate the shrapnel of a 12-gauge buck-eye, on our front porch. Paired with the weight of the life she left behind, we carried her casket together a few weeks later over white pea gravel to her final resting place.

Disbelief had run rampant across all of the civil service departments. They had all but closed the city down, every fire engine and ambulance from across the tri-county area was there. The air ambulances flew overhead, and we wept. The guttural weeping of the likes I had never known.

In a compromise with Sue's father, even though she had been an atheist, the family clergyman dredged us along with his choice of scripture. With a transitional shudder, I checked out of my body. I was floating above myself. Higher and higher I rose.

Both parts of me were conscious and aware of visceral processes happening. In other words, even in this split, there was no escaping the pain. As I ascended, I could feel the blazing sun against my back. Like Icarus, I was too close to the sun, and my resilience was melting faster than wax. The words, "your son needs you," whispered in my ear would bring me back together with a slam.

Well-meaning friends and family one by one walked by with the best words and tokens of love that they could muster.

BEYOND BOUNDARIES: THRIVING IN LIFE'S GREY ZONE

"I'm so sorry for your loss, she's not suffering anymore, if you need anything..." Each sound, each tickle of hot breath against my ears felt like a brillo pad agitating my frayed nerves in the worst way. My secrets being buried under a mound of goodbyes.

Foolishly I had believed that I could keep them buried far below the surface of the naked eye. Afterall, no one really cared about the truth, or knew how to process any of it. The lack of emotional processing had been the missing ingredient the entire time. Sue was the fourth paramedic to take her own life that year in our small community. I refused to share the full story, and have her remembered as anything less than a hero, because that was the truth of her life.

It has been thirteen years, so why now you ask? I am no longer naive enough to believe that my truth is any less important to be shared, or that the full truth takes away from the heroism of our lives. My son is grown, with children of his own. Legacy is carried on the wings of vulnerability, and authenticity. Their destination is freedom, and we are all worthy of the experience.

These are the untold chapters of mental health stigma and how the consequences unfolded in our lives.

Like a baby during a colic relieving car ride, she was asleep within minutes. Her body had been through the ringer and there were still remnant effects of the barbiturates, anxiety medications and sleeping meds that she had taken. A count of around 300, that she had ingested with alcohol to paint the picture better. All of the above exited her body, creating a pungent pool in the floorboard of the car.

She wouldn't wake up for 6-7 hours. It took me 4 of them to slowly drag her from the car to the house. My 5ft, 2 inch frame was no match to her 6 feet of dead weight. She had brief moments of lucidity, when she would threaten me verbally. I didn't antagonize her, I knew she was serious, but at the same time, I ridiculously felt safe in my own mind. She couldn't even keep her eyes open! In the moments of her being out cold, I took action steps for the safety of us both.

I went through the house and bagged up every medication and supplement we had. I put them quietly in the dryer, not three feet from where she laid. We were house sitting for our landlords next door at the time. I had also removed the one firearm in our possession to their house. I had masterfully hidden it in their spare craft room underneath the mattress of the bed. I had done this as quickly as lightning so that she wouldn't wake up and find that I was gone.

We were well into the first 24 hours. I had managed to get her cleaned and into new clothes. The dried activated charcoal was like chiseling concrete off of a rose petal. She was beginning to stir more frequently and with more vigor. Her threats were becoming more intense. I personally called a private EMS service that Sue worked for to have her transferred to a different hospital than before, believing that they would surely keep her this time.

Again, the systems in place failed us both. Sue would act right as rain in the presence of hospital staff. She would answer their questions, smile even. When they exited the room her entire demeanor would change and she would begin to threaten me; sneering, snarling, and even growling. When I went into the hallway to discuss her behavior with the nurse, Sue faked a seizure. They knew that she was faking, but they gave her valium anyway. This was to aid in calming her down, so that I could manage her until the facility she needed to be admitted into had an opening. This was said to be approximately two days away.

It was past nightfall again. She was awake and aware now. The IV fluids they had given her had aided in her returning to a normal physical state. She had taken the keys as soon as we were outside of the hospital doors. She drove to a little taco fast food joint and we ordered food through the drive thru. I wasn't hungry; I was numb and afraid. How was I in this situation? I felt the cliche of a Lifetime movie.

She drove us to a park and we sat under a tree. "Eat" she commanded, "this is our last meal baby." I choked the lumps of food down as large crocodile tears ceaselessly flowed down my face, drenching the top of my shirt. All the while my brain was scanning, analyzing, and evaluating for any moment that would serve as a gateway out.

I also want to add that Sue was under a medical doctor's care for her depression, and anxiety. We had been advised to follow through on cognitive behavior therapy and other modalities that were blown off and seen as beneath the realm of what was going to be helpful by her, by Sue.

I thought I had known what it felt like to want something so badly you would give anything to receive it. I thought I knew what it felt like to have that something in your grasp and have it slip away. I thought I knew a lot of things. I thought I had talked her down, changed her mind. She finally seemed calm and convinced me she had[SD3] returned to her senses. I was so very tired. Though I knew she could be lying, my eyes betrayed me, and closed for one second. I felt her climb into the bed beside me and lay down.

Like a jack-in-the-box she sprang up, "Where is the gun?" she growled furiously. She began ransacking the house looking everywhere. I was sitting up on the bed, but I was in the fetal position, all the same. Pure terror was pulsing through my body.

I began to pray and plead with the universe. "You took it over there didn't you?" She left out the back door heading to the neighbor's house where I had earlier hidden it.

I grabbed the keys to the car that I had managed to wrestle away from her earlier and also hid. I ran through the house and out the front door. I slowed down, and shut the car door quietly. My hands were shaking uncontrollably, I dropped the keys on the floor board. Oh no, no, no! I reached down to grab them and as I rose back up, the rearview mirror revealed to me an image that I will never forget. In the dim moonlight, stood the solid silhouette of someone I did not recognize in the least with a shotgun, pointed at me, and I began to sob out my love for my son and my family. I could see my life running through the hourglass of existence. I accepted my fate as she opened the car door.

There are defining moments in our life when we have seismic shifts in our understanding of things outside of causality. You see, fate is something predetermined; all at once, as we walked back through the house and she was telling me how "fast and painless" it would be, I knew destiny was what I chose. When she turned around and our eyes met, where a fawn had been, a mother empowered by survival instincts now stood.

"I'm a little teapot short and stout. Here is my handle, here is my spout. When I get all steamed up, hear me shout! Tip me over and pour me out." I sang this as a child. I was boiling mad, and it surged through my veins, swelling my muscles with massive strength. I managed to get the gun away and cram it between the mattresses where I sat over it. Bubbling questions were on the rise. Was I going to have to use the gun myself? I began praying even harder. "Please, release me," I begged.

Sue, too, was maniacally seeking an escape. In a moment that met both of our needs in the most symbolic of ways, both of our most wanted desires were delivered at the same time. In her desperation she had walked out into the hallway, slamming the door so hard that the door facing came unhinged and I physically heard "Now! Run!" I didn't hesitate, like a coiled rattlesnake I was up and over her and outside, this time "rattling" as it were, no longer being silent, but crying and yelling as I ran.

Rattlesnakes have a remarkable adaptability to their own venom; as I entered the gray zone, I learned that we as humans do, too. Persian poet, Hafiz, wrote, "Do not surrender your grief so quickly. Let it cut more deeply. Let it season you the way few Human or Divine ingredients can." I did, intuitively in every way in the months and years to follow. I didn't hide my struggle or my pain. I wore it in the form of a razors edge on my skin. I drank it in the form of alcohol. I tasted it with nicotine, drugs and food.

I felt it, in the form of a sexual assault some four months later, having been drugged by Sue's lover's partner whom I had sought out for revenge. I danced with grief, and it burned me deeply enough to demand that I choose death myself or create a new identity.

Creating the courage to look deeply within is an enthralling experience. When we look through the veil of cosmic illusion and lay our resistance down, we become open to receive grief's message: there is no death, only transformation. Every tear that we cry is a dazzling story, and the return of the Soul Love that lies deep within the limitless waves of our compassionate hearts. Though it feels as if we will but wither away, the ocean is plentiful and our spirit does not perish.

Death, just as empathy and love, makes all equal. It makes every moment precious. The uncertainty of its time can free us from procrastination. Free us from the illusion that we can keep putting off living until a future time. The earnest thoughts of one's own death can liberate us from the layers and masks we wear. I chose to reinvent myself. Something that I now do by free will daily, through creating my own joy and freedoms.

Today, I help entrepreneurs create brands that are authentic and beautifully crafted from their core passions. I live audaciously, giving others the permission to do the same. My son is also a paramedic and entrepreneur. We are survivors, forged in the fire and reimagined into thriving individuals, living our best lives.

If you or someone you know is suffering with forms of depression, post-traumatic stress syndrome, anxiety, grief and thoughts of self-harm, know that you are not alone. YOU can thrive in the gray. It is difficult at times to see and listen through the murk of ourselves. There is nothing wrong with you, only pain that needs processing through skills that you do not yet have. Or, perhaps miscommunication between the chemicals in your brain and body. If you remember only one thing from this chapter, remember to breathe!

Your breath is the body's way to communicate safety to your brain, whether your body feels it is safe or not. This will allow you to access your executive function and make decisions that can support you in living. Your breath will also help you to restore your body in any recovery. Breath with me now, in through your nose for 1,2,3,4. Hold at the top for 1,2,3,4,5,6,7. Finally, exhale for 1,2,3,4,5,6,7,8. You're doing great! You really do have a one hundred percent success rate.

Meet Jenny Ford, the powerhouse behind Uniqua New Beauty Norm L.L.C., The L.A.B.E.L. Branding Academy, and Avant-Garde Branding Systems. She's a certified coaching rockstar, author, speaker, human rights consultant, makeup guru, and stylist extraordinaire. She also spends her free time mentoring the future fierce leaders of the world. One mustn't forget, she is also Supreme Queen of the Unicorns. Reach out to me for further tips and a road map for how we heal via email at thedeeperseasoning@gmail.com.

To my dearest son,
In you, I found the true meaning of unconditional love and boundless joy. This chapter is dedicated to you, my constant source of inspiration and strength. Your laughter fills my heart with warmth, and your strength is always awe inspiring. Know that no matter where life takes you, my love will always be a steadfast anchor, guiding you through both calm waters and stormy seas. May you always chase your dreams with courage, kindness, and integrity, and may each chapter of your life be filled with endless adventures and profound discoveries.
With all my love,
Mom

Lights Out... How to Manage the Unexpected

By: Marlene Foster

Travelers drag aching feet through pitch black darkness while light closes its heavy eyelids to embrace change. I hear footsteps. Do you? Voices echo tirelessly, searching through a winding maze of tunnels. The view becomes darker with a spot of light. Discomfort can be beneficial, yet unsettling when fear entangles progress. Change deepens the healing and suffering of a throbbing wound. Meanwhile, courageous hearts dare to step beyond the boundaries. Will you?

Uncertainty may cause outcomes that communities have no control over. Yet, there's still a way to choose positive over a negative outlook. Envision the next step. On the other hand, there will be times when options become available. Make a choice and continue to update viable options. Anticipate. Make changes that strengthen the outcome, minimize damage and also pursue uncertainty.

During the pandemic, long lines wrapped around global communities, seeking remedies. Businesses shut down or transformed products and services. Unemployment peaked and businesses lost large numbers of employees.

How Does Uncertainty Influence You

The unknown has a continuous rhythm of change that fluctuates up and down. You never know what's coming next. Stay ready to enact a courageous action plan. If there's nothing in place, remain flexible with an inventive mindset.

One direction may be taken to achieve an overwhelming

victory, and another to minimize defeat. How about considering the grey area? What if the middle road dared you to step outside the boundaries to engage uncertainty? For centuries, women chose natural childbirth. Today, expectant mothers give birth at home, in birth centers or at the hospital.

Pregnancies rely exclusively upon the medical profession. Expectant mothers may also include herbal remedies, daily exercise, and a healthy diet. My daughter chose a healthy lifestyle, yet experienced a high risk pregnancy. She ate kiwi, pomegranate, grapes and other quality fruit. Her diet included tasty meals like spinach, grilled salmon and carrots–including a healthy dose of Omega 3.

Sometimes there's a choice, and at other times, no option. Expectant mothers may have the opportunity to receive a c-section or vaginal birth. In both cases, a 100% guarantee would not exist. How can doctors predict a perfect delivery, or a baby's life span?

I'm grateful for the time spent with my three year old granddaughter and doubly grateful for the granddaughter whom I had a chance to enjoy for a brief period of time. Unexpected outcomes challenge families as well as businesses. Adversity has begun to strengthen resilience.

Prepare for the unexpected. Keep an umbrella near the doorway, ready to protect against a downpour. Don't forget to place a spare tire and jack in the trunk of the car.

You can't plan for everything. Therefore, try to develop an adaptable mindset. I will always remember the joyful moments spent with a beautiful little angel. My heart aches while sitting here writing about her. The beautiful pictures and stories describing my granddaughter bring incredible joy. Each day I reminisce, show gratitude and am starting to accept change.

Does Risk Promote Value?

Some businesses discover how to guard against uncertainty and others simply toss a coin and hope for the best. How possible would it be to protect a business against every storm? On the other hand, how safe would it be to stand in the middle of the road facing the unknown? From a distance, trucks appear to travel at a high rate of speed.

That would be similar to a little girl running down the sidewalk watching every step in order to prevent a fall, or running carelessly down the middle of the street. More than likely, she'll return home bruised from head to toe. Perfection doesn't exist. Although, there's no need to proceed recklessly.

Unknown pathways invite you to step outside the boundaries. I've spent years working long hours to build a business, skipping meals and sleep while caring for a young child; success eventually came. Enrich life with wisdom, gratitude and resilience.

Families want the best for their children. Health insurance offers unexpected protection. Will illness occur overnight, or while little ones are away at school? Parents discover healthy meals, activities and beverages that reinforce a healthy mind and body. Moreover, it's great knowing that the medical profession can be relied upon, as well as freedom to boost a healthy lifestyle.

Consider risks that influence value and moments of discomfort, such as adding new skills to the business. For example, podcasting has gained enormous popularity. Writing a book may be time consuming, yet large quantities of books are being produced.

Great planning may or may not bring an expected value. Nevertheless, it's best to continuously update and make changes to safeguard assets. What's the possibility of leadership dying from a brain tumor? The company may later discover that the successor lacked expertise needed to assume full responsibility of an executive role. What's next?

How to Plan for Protection

Plan now to safeguard the family with mortgage protection, college planning and death protection. What if the husband has an unexpected injury on the job and required long term disability? How would the family cover finances? Most life policies have short and long term coverage.

Businesses can receive coverage that will pay overhead expenses. Now's the time to discover and implement contingency plans. Remember to keep the plan updated. I recall hearing a man speak of multiple family and business plans he owned and how he'd forgotten to remove his ex-wife from the beneficiary section.

Businesses sometimes experience a professional decision to terminate employment. A buy-sell agreement will give remaining partners the resources needed for replacement. The agreement will also give a severance package to the exiting partner. Uncertainty can occur at any hour, day or night. I became injured on the job. Fortunately, employee group coverage was in place. Think about it. How would you protect your family and the business?

Transformation - Face to Face with Uncertainty

At the start of the pandemic, I'd never interviewed before and decided to make a career change. Podcast interviews shared global business experiences, employee terminations and resignations. Many interviewees became business owners and authors. I'm also writing a book. Since the pandemic, what type of changes have you made?

During the Great Resignation, businesses were left empty handed. Employees felt undervalued. Looking abroad, I was impressed with countries who incentivized and encouraged development throughout the organization. They sacrificed and serviced employee and customer needs. Businesses networked and developed communities all over the world. Servant leadership stepped forward to listen, empathize, team and empower worldwide.

Prior to the pandemic, I was accustomed to traveling nonstop to conduct business face to face. A transformation took place, preparing me for the future. I teamed with businesses all over the world on a weekly podcast to develop visibility. Together we shared stories of how stepping beyond the boundaries can lead to adversity and success.

Leadership may feel uncomfortable planning for a direct replacement. Think of the benefits. Succession planning has helped to guard against unexpected termination because it initiated training and employee achievement. This great strategy helped businesses to minimize cost as there's no need to invest in recruitment.

Employees develop strong leadership skills that promote growth and diligence, enabling them to manage the business. If by chance leadership became disabled or decided to sell, prospective buyers would be excited by the business expertise and value displayed. At retirement, owners would have little difficulty selling a reputable business that has the ability to stand on its own.

The Effects of Disrepair: What Next?

Businesses resemble families. Circumstances occur within a department that affect not only a key employee, but the entire team. When setbacks occur, utilize the company plan and implement more advanced revisions. Be resourceful.

Continue to make progress. Look ahead to anticipate uncertainty. If a fire occurred and the smoke detector malfunctioned, what would be the next plan of action? If the umbrella kept at the front door now has a hole in it, you can rely on the one left at the office or on the backset of the car.

Solopreneurs face deep challenges when operating without a backup plan. Since the pandemic, many have collaborated, joined memberships and now mentor professional teams. Leadership benefits by teaming within the business community.

Years ago, I was conducting business in the office with a client and sweat began to roll down my forehead, cheeks and neck. Unbelievable. My hands felt grimy and feverish. Moisture splashed all over the paperwork, smearing printed documents—felt as if I was sitting near a fiery furnace. The humble client rushed to make a phone call for me. Another professional hurried over to complete the transaction, and took me to the hospital. The illness turned out to be pneumonia. I asked the doctor to reaffirm the diagnosis because I never get sick!

Did I lose clients?

Yes. Some faced emergencies and needed immediate assistance. Others called to check on my progress. Today, I have a plan of action that's reviewed, revised and reassessed by a team. How often should businesses make changes? As often as needed.

Discover more effective ways to safeguard the business. Evaluate possible outcomes. There will be times when change became unnerving, fearing that a new method may not be the best option. Attend workshops, seminars, read books, conduct surveys, and invite a team of professionals to share quality experiences. Valuable experiences can also be gained through a high quality mentorship. Also, conduct workshops: teach and learn from class participants.

Take a test drive.

Team up and discuss planning with other community leaders. Use some of the strategies within the business. Consider how the plan would benefit a business that met an unexpected setback. Interview businesses and share quality experiences. Invite listeners to ask questions and engage in detailed discussions. Collaboration empowers the community.

Protection Beyond the Boundaries

Consider the following story that I wrote on Quora. What if a business conflict triggered a series of events that a spousal partnership had not anticipated? This would have a major impact on the business. There would be at least three challenges.

Brown and Associates were crushed to hear that a key employee, who manufactured specialty furniture for the past 20 years, had died. Neither husband nor wife knew of any other employee with this unique craftsmanship. The man's expertise had given the company an exclusive brand in the industry. What would they do now? Most importantly, what should they have done before now?

Businesses must plan and update contingency plans. Death does tend to be a top candidate for uncertainty. The

Browns needed life insurance on themselves and key employees. Protection would have strengthened trust and profitability among executives, employees, customers, and the community. The tax-free benefit could have been used to recruit a professional who would step in to help run the business, or pay a business successor who would have been trained and ready to move forward. Brown and Associates could also use the tax free death benefit to level or balance costs that wouldn't have normally been in place prior to the employee's death.

Succession planning would help to prepare for death, disability, termination, divorce etc. With a key employee or partner trained and ready to take on a leadership role, a setback wouldn't cause an unexpected disruption in business. Exit planning would occur when owners prepare for a future sale and promotion of professionals into new business roles.

For years, Mr. Brown thought about selling the business to another merchant. He and his wife could then start a winery. Mrs. Brown agreed with her husband that the business should be sold, but she always wanted to invest in imported home furnishings. The business was an extension of Mr. Brown's family legacy. Unfortunately, the family agreed with Mrs. Brown, and the decision was made in her favor.

How would a succession plan have saved the business, and maybe a marriage? Training sharpens skills and prepares professionals to step into the shoes of upper management. In addition, a buy-sell agreement would protect the business brand in case the partnership or marriage was terminated. Specific guidelines would be included with updates.

New professionals should have been brought into the business much sooner to gain exposure and manufacture their own one-of-a-kind creations. Family members with similar experiences could have also collaborated with talented professionals. On the other hand, a more affordable approach would have been to train a company successor who would have been ready to continue the company's operations with originality.

An Unexpected Detour

Since the marriage has taken a different turn, this does appear to cause an even greater rip. Even with a spousal partnership, strategies may still create a succession plan for business continuation. Divorce or death should be planned for, along with continuous updates. Look beyond what's in place today. Lack of immediate business action impacts the family, organization, employees, and customers.

In the event of a divorce, a buy-sell agreement could determine beforehand who would maintain the business, while the spouses agree upon an equitable consideration. In this situation, it may be probable that even if the family decided on Mrs. Brown's proposition, she would still be the one to leave and accept the monetary terms. A buy-sell agreement would be an excellent option for showing current and future business distribution.

Whether an unexpected termination, illness, death or retirement occurs, businesses would keep the document updated beyond the start date. Those who had a buy-sell agreement in place prior to the pandemic most likely minimized damages. For continuous protection, companies would continue to update the terms with more advanced strategies.

Death: Fixable or Adaptable Mindset

Brown and Associates failed to plan for themselves or a key employee.

What's Fixable?

An organization should protect the business, families, employees, customers and community with exceptional business planning that creates a progressive strategy. Don't allow the plan to snooze. Keep it updated. Encourage employees to contribute. Inclusive environments benefit extensively when they invite innovative ideas. Employees add exceptional value when they're held to high expectations. Training has taken place and teams will be ready to perform.

Adaptable Mindset

What if a death occurred in the marital partnership? There would be both fixable and adaptable solutions in place along with a buy-sell agreement giving the surviving spouse ownership of the business shares. With an agreement in place, the family business still may have caused the wife to experience limitations in a family owned business. Although, without an agreement, the outcome most definitely would not have been in Mrs. Brown's favor.

In addition, the spouses needed to enhance emotional intelligence within their marriage and throughout the business. The Browns would have faced an overwhelming challenge, being forced to meet death's untimely outcome. Death of a spouse would hopefully cause the organization to empower one another. Understanding how employees would also be affected by death creates an empathetic mindset. Implement these simple tips.

- Self-awareness – be aware of emotions
- Help the entire company to accept change and to promote new experiences
- Just like a skill that's being learned, trust yourself and know that each day is a new day.

In Conclusion...

Be proactive in personal and business matters. Think of a plan and backup plan that would safeguard a personal and business lifestyle. Contingency plans prepare businesses to step in the right direction. If they fail, create revisions that make the foundation stronger.

You can't plan everything...

Two months ago, my daughter delivered a beautiful baby girl. She died two weeks ago. Each step has been helpful, but overwhelmingly painful. Thanks for being here alongside me to hear how unexpected challenges can impact both the personal and business mindset. I'm gradually moving back towards the business and writing a book that I've been working on for a few months.

"Come be inspired. Let's empower one another. Join the weekly post, '500 Moments of Discomfort' on Linkedin. In 2024, I'm looking to introduce 500 stories! Share moments that overwhelmingly led to amazing growth. See you there!"

Empower The Vision enriches global visibility by spotlighting business expertise, and growth, and protecting unexpected challenges (termination, death, long-term illness and divorce). One-on-one, group consultations and workshops demonstrate protection strategies. The content encourages roleplay, public speaking and peer review.

My background includes 20+ years of consulting, business protection, public speaking, sales, marketing, insurance, and writing business articles. I coach and engage quality relationships that impact family protection, employee relations, customer loyalty, and community awareness. Participants develop buy-sell agreements and contingency plans to guard against unexpected challenges. Relationship-building creates growth and trustworthiness for startups and existing businesses. Interviewees introduce expertise, published works, and social media content.

After being part of a family business that was liquidated, I discovered ways to anticipate the unexpected and safeguard family, employees, customers, and assets. I now build a legacy that impacts today and tomorrow. Grandmother developed strong customer relationships. As the result of an incurable illness, a profitable business that could have been sold was liquidated.

https://linkedin.com/in/marlene-foster-b841339b #500momentsofdiscomfort.

As a result of the pandemic, the decline in face-to-face connections, business closures, and unemployment caused businesses worldwide to engage in podcasts. My daughter's content review and video editing made the posts and podcasts phenomenal. Collaboration led to guests making more and more referrals. Also, my upcoming book will introduce the incredible Spotlight Team.

Authors introduced upcoming books and previous publications of new authors. Male-owned businesses endorse female aspiring authors and small businesses. My post, Women With a Winners Perception, has attracted female and male business owners.

I'm hosting this year's 2024 business membership and program. Sponsors support and engage team-building strategies for startups. Community awareness empowers both leadership and startups.

I sponsor an amazing post, Writers Who Wow. Authors empower one another through books, online posts and book reviews and referrals to spotlight influential thought leaders. The 2024 Author membership includes local authors marketing content face-to-face.

I'd like to thank all of these wonderful contributors who continue to make a difference.

Burning desire – Making my dreams come true

By: Timothy Gleeson

I want everyone to know that we can make our biggest dreams come true. My dream was to obtain a business diploma followed by a university degree. I put all of my energy and efforts into daily routines and had the courage to take greater risks. I believed in myself, in the hope of achieving something greater than I ever thought possible, to live a better life and provide more for my family. A mindset with the expectation of succeeding despite the challenges was my way to get there. My hope is that you can take my story and apply it in a way that will make it work for you to make your dreams come true. We never know what we are capable of until forced to deal with a situation we are in, or a burning desire to be who we dreamed to become.

There is no magic pill in life. Rather it's hard work, digging in, and taking some calculated risks, with only yourself to blame if things go wrong. However, you should also take the credit when things go your way and celebrate those successes. How we see ourselves in our minds determines how happy and how successful we become. Positive self-talk is so important, and visualizing ourselves achieving our goals can be life changing if we follow through by consistently applying meaningful efforts over time.

In the 1980's, I left high school ready to go to university, hoping to become a primary school teacher. However, my helping someone by working over the Christmas holidays led to a full-time job where the pay was too good to refuse. I had been saving for five years with many part-time jobs in the hope of saving enough for a deposit for a two-bedroom apartment. Interest rates were high as was inflation and property prices were also increasing. I was worried that by spending three years studying full time, I would miss the opportunity to purchase a property.

For the next fifteen years I worked in middle management roles in warehousing, logistics and convenience stores. It seemed that to get promoted to a senior management role you either needed a university degree qualification or you knew someone in the industry you were applying.

I changed direction and became self-employed as a Sydney Taxi Driver, working twelve-hour shifts, five to six days each week. It was one of the toughest jobs I had ever experienced even though the money was good. The downside was I had no quality time with my young family.

I had been asked to take a day off work to attend a friend's daughter's university graduation ceremony. I was indifferent to the event, thinking my time could be better spent working and earning money from driving my taxi. I tagged along as my wife insisted, I go, as it was to show face to her Chinese friends.

I was seated on the left-hand side, halfway up in the auditorium. I quickly realized everything was very formal and somewhat regal with the ceremony. All those academics wearing their robes, big hats, and what I can only describe as a man with a Gandalf walking stick, appeared on the stage, then took their seats. There were several speeches and then the award ceremony began calling the graduates in alphabetical order, according to their accreditation. After a student's name was called, they walked up a platform of stairs to an official, shook their hand while receiving their degree, and then exited the stage back to their seat.

I was mesmerized by the atmosphere, and it occurred to me that it was public recognition of an academic achievement. As the ceremony ended, I vowed to myself that one day I would be one of those university graduates receiving a degree. I didn't know how, but once I had this burning desire, I would set a pathway in motion.

I specifically dreamed of seeing myself receiving a degree at a university graduation ceremony. Not once, but many times over five years. I kept my dream private because of the fear that others would see me as crazy.

As an early adult, obtaining direct entry for a university placement was next to impossible. However, I worked out a pathway to get there to complete a Business Diploma through Technical & Further Education (TAFE).

When I was planning to complete my Diploma of Business Studies at TAFE, I had to work out how I could coordinate studying full-time while also earning enough money to meet our mortgage repayments on our home loan and being there for my family with two young children. I didn't know how difficult the study would be or how much time I would need to complete my studies to pass.

Most full-time students live at home with their parents or live on campus, perhaps with a part-time job. I had no such luxury, making the odds stacked against me. But I wanted a better life than being cramped in a vehicle for twelve hours and coming home too tired to enjoy a happy life with my family.

Rather than talk me out of it, I kept visualizing that

university graduation ceremony and thought of practical ways to make it work. I talked to myself every day like a coach encouraging their players to perform their personal best on the field. My goal was to complete my weekly study, Monday to Thursday, and then drive three taxi shifts from Friday to Sunday. I had the support of my wife, who took care of our home and children. I had a mindset of success and just needed to get on with it.

A typical study day would involve waking up early and helping my wife prepare breakfast for everyone. I would then catch a bus to TAFE to attend classes and return home to do my homework before bathing the kids and sitting down for the family dinner. We would then get the kids to sleep, and I would do further study.

The content of the Business Diploma was a mixture of management, marketing, human resources, accounting, economics, and project management.

There were also individual assignments, group assignments, mid semester exams and final exams. What favored me was having fifteen years of actual work experience, which meant I could apply so many life experiences to my assignments to confirm my understanding of the subject matter. I made it all work through setting consistent routines, which made it manageable.

A subject that was difficult for me was Business Statistics. I sat at the front of the class, and I couldn't grasp the content. I reached out to my teacher, requesting help. She assisted me by giving me additional work and further guidance. For the final three-hour exam, I sat in the class's back row to feel less distracted. After the first hour more than half of the 30 students had given up and left the room, but I didn't panic and just kept working through the exam paper. With an hour to go I looked up and realized I was the only student left in the room. I glanced at the supervisor, and he said to me, "You're it, and you have an hour left." I apologized and said I will need this last hour. I finished my paper with five minutes to go and felt exhausted. I was so proud of myself for having passed this subject.

Towards the end of my diploma, my accounting teacher advised me to enroll in a Business Degree at the University of Technology (UTS), Broadway Campus, as she thought I would be a great accountant. I had mixed feelings because, as I explained to her, while my results were good, I spent double my time with accounting because the concepts were hard to understand, and I preferred Management & Human Resources subjects. The other advantage was UTS would give me four subject exemptions, which was the equivalent of a full semester.

I completed my Diploma of Business Studies in two years in December 2000 with a Distinction average.

I started university in February 2001 - a Bachelor of Business. The scary thing was a high school leaver needed to be in the top 15% UAI for this degree, which I was well below when I finished high school. It was so different compared to TAFE, where the pace was much faster. It seemed every class was overbooked. My first lecture had every seat taken, with students sitting on the side steps and others standing on the side. During this time all lectures and tutorials were conducted on campus with no facility for distance learning.

In the second week we could all sit in a seat in the lecture hall and by the fourth week they were asking students to move closer to the front. The dropout rate was phenomenal. It seemed there was no order, only chaos. I remember in my first law lecture the Professor said look at the person on each side of you, the person in front, and the person behind you. At graduation three of those four students would have dropped out. Not a confidence boost I was hoping for.

By week six I was ready to drop out.

However, I sought the advice from my Human Resources TAFE Teacher, Susan Coleman. Her advice was this: Tim, University is 20% intelligence and 80% perseverance. So go to every lecture and pay attention, go to every tutorial seeking answers for the things you don't understand from the supervisor, do all your homework, read every reading because it was examinable, hand in your assignments on time, and sit every exam. Do these things for your 24 subjects and you will get your degree.

The other piece of advice was that Universities don't care if you pass or fail. They don't care if you don't turn up, but they will mark your attendance. If you don't progress by passing subjects, they will send you warning letters stating potential suspension or expulsion. Financially, the university debt follows you through the tax system.

With Susan's advice, I then organized my game plan. It was a very similar plan that I used to obtain my Business Diploma. With four subjects a semester, I allocated four days of the week to attend the lectures and tutorials and complete homework, assignments, and exams. The other three days were allocated to driving my taxi in 12-hour shifts from 3 am – 3pm. Time management was key, so I developed daily routines to get me through.

There were many group assignments because the accounting industry requires collaboration and the ability to work in teams. I formed my first accounting study team choosing a guy sitting next to me by the name of Robin. I also recognized this tall guy from TAFE. From a distance, I yelled out, "Big Mike!". Mike turned around and called me "Big Tim"; the name has always stuck with me. Robin invited his friend Tracey, and we became known as the "Big Team."

The funny thing is the name is contradictory because I am not big at all. I stand just a little over five feet tall, but I do have a big heart.

We divided the work, agreed on dates to follow up, reviewed, and then submitted the group assignment on time. It worked so well that we followed each other in the same tutorials so we could form the same team in other subjects. We remain great friends to this day.

My university experiences also had its moments. In the second semester of my second year, I was hit by a van after putting two steps from the curb on a busy road. The impact threw me forward, but to the side, so I was lucky the van didn't run over me.

Realizing I was still on the road my flight or fight response compelled me to get up and I took 10 steps to get to the footpath. An ambulance was called, and I was informed I had a fractured right leg with my torso heavily bruised. How can someone walk on a fractured leg and not feel any pain? The doctor explained it was adrenaline kicking in. Just extraordinary. My leg in a brace for the next twelve weeks. It was hard to move. Was this a sign telling me to give up?

I contacted the university to explain what happened, and I withdrew from one subject. I was given special permission to study from home with the other three subjects because they were assignment-based, and there was just one subject with a final exam, which I arranged to attend.

I completed my Business Degree (a major in accounting & sub-major in small business Accounting) with a Credit average in three years. It was surreal. I had achieved my dream.

Six months prior to obtaining my Business Degree, I sought guidance from a university career counselor. After I informed him, I was older than thirty years of age, he told me that no accounting firm would employ me. It was crushing news I was too old. The Big Four accounting firms were geared to hire and train young twenty-something university graduating students with a view to an entry level starting salary package. Not some thirty-something aspirant hoping to slide in with a middle-management starting salary. The advice was to find someone I knew in the industry who would give me a start.

I knew several people in the industry, but I had to be creative with my approach. Something far more beneficial to them to help me get my foot in the door.

I had a school friend who worked in the accounting & tax industry. It just so happened that several times I picked him up from taxi stands to various places. It helped that he graduated from the same university where I was studying, and I told him of my progress during the taxi ride.

At a school reunion, I suggested a proposal that I work

two days a week for free for the next six months, and if he were happy with my progress, then I would be offered a full-time role.

I was financially able to offer this as I was more motivated to obtain the necessary experience in something I had never done before. My friend told me he had to discuss this proposal with the other business partners and would get back to me.

Fast forward a month, and I was informed they would put me on a six-month trial with an agreement of a full-time position if I satisfied their requirements. Rather than work unpaid, I was to supply tax invoices at an agreed rate for the six-month trial as a contractor. This was much better than I expected, and I always wonder if my offer to work for six months free was a deciding factor. What I did know was that businesses only advertise for vacant positions if they are unable to fill a role from their network of contacts. There was already an establishment of trust and I kept saying to myself to give it my best shot.

Six months passed, and I was offered a full-time position.

I then sought a professional accounting accreditation while working full-time as a taxation accountant. For three years, I applied my efforts to the Institute of Chartered Accountants Australia (ICAA) program. I passed the taxation module but failed the other five modules several times. During this period, my father died unexpectedly, which affected my concentration.

However, I never gave up. I looked for another pathway to my future. I transferred to the CPA Australia program and again I dreamed of receiving my professional accounting accreditation in another ceremony.

After studying three hours each night, Monday through Friday and on weekends, I became a member of CPA Australia after two and a half years, and I had another very proud moment in 2010.

There is always hope if we can dream it and put those thoughts into action.

I was lucky with my taxi driving situation. I worked for an operator who had a fleet of 50 vehicles, so there was capacity for me to add to and cut back my shifts, provided I gave a week's notice in advance. I could reduce my shifts when exams were coming and work extra shifts between semesters.

The taxi industry was based on a bailment agreement between a taxi operator and myself as the driver. Each day or night shift had a set rate that you paid for the use of the vehicle for those twelve hours. The other costs were the LPG gas and tolls. On average, I would need to make $150.00 per shift to cover the above costs, and what I made over and above was my taxable income.

During my studying periods after driving a 12-hour shift, I was too exhausted to do any study. I also had to assist my wife with preparing the kids for bath time, dinner, and getting them to go to sleep. My aim was to be in bed by 8 pm so I could wake up at 2 am, and then begin my 12-hour shift at 3 am.

The power of dreams and visualizing what we want to become is real, and it can be achieved by the energy we direct toward applying practical measures in a way that gives us the best chance of succeeding. It's best not to over think it, and instead get in there and do what you can with the belief that it will work. Celebrate every win. Talk to yourself and don't compare yourself with anyone because it is your driven single mindedness that will get you to become who you dream to be.

I am passionate about all things tax for small business, to include producing financial statements and provide advice for companies, trusts, partnerships and SMSF's, including income tax returns & tax returns for individuals as a Tax Agent & CPA.

I changed my career 20 years ago through obtaining a Business Diploma and then a Business Degree, having extensive management experience in warehousing and distribution, convenience store and self-employment as a taxi driver.

I am a property investor in the Sydney property market. I serve voluntarily on the committees of these Owner Corporations. I am also passionate about a few things close to my heart, such as cancer, mental health, and specifically suicide prevention. I am against any form of bullying, and my purpose is kindness.

My favorite activity is surfing, where most of my problems are solved in those quiet moments, waiting for the next wave.

More Than a Victim

By: Jackie Hallberg, LMSW

Today I work with those that commit crimes and those that have been victimized, and I have for more than 20 years now. Who would have thought that life would come full circle as I experienced my own victimization back in high school. It is a significant part of my life that I have rarely shared with anyone, let alone never written about before this book.

I wasn't the pretty or athletic girl in high school. I was smart, but didn't stand out in any way. My high school was tiny so everyone knew each other, most of us tolerated everyone and there were only a few people that were in cliques. I felt like I could talk to everyone. I loved everything about school until the weekend of my assault.

My main friendship circle was split between a few different groups. Each group did mostly different things but it was still small town fun when we went out. One of the groups was mostly older girls who were a bit more into partying. Partying back in the day before there were cell phones and social media pages was so much different than it is today...when any decision you make in what is supposed to be the safety of your friends could be posted and change the rest of your life in ways I was fortunate not to experience. However, being out with friends doesn't always protect you from other harm.

Now, teenagers are hurt not just once, but a million times over when they see their victimization spread across social media. Seeing other people, many who are strangers yet some they had considered friends all sharing or laughing videos and pictures that were taken at their most intimate times. Although technology is a great thing, I hurt so badly for those with images online that they wish were never taken as now they have a permanent reminder of the evil that happened to them. I strive to make sure anyone hurting from those posts knows they are valued and worthy of thriving beyond the impact those images made on them.

Some of what I am about to share should be read with the understanding of a trigger warning. If you continue reading and anything makes you relive your assault or gives you thoughts of self-harm or suicide, please seek help from a professional immediately. You deserve to heal from what you have been through, just as I have healed. My assault happened over 30 years ago, and I avoided even thinking about it until rather recently. Please don't wait as long as I did!

High school years are filled with so much angst while we are all trying to find ourselves. Yet I knew from an early age that I was meant to help kids! I planned to go to college to get into the helping field, even though I had no idea the foreshadowing those thoughts would bring to both help myself and so many others after my assault.

Keep in mind, back when my assault happened there was no "me too" movement, there were no counselors in schools and women still weren't holding high ranking positions. I had high hopes to make the world a better place, yet after my assault, I questioned my ability to help others when I felt I wore a label across my face that said, "damaged." Back then, I would have never realized just how much I could thrive and grow to help others. This was because no one ever helped me through my journey.

It began as just another weekend party with someone securing a keg. A few of us headed to the wooded field that the party was being hosted at that night. Yes, we were all underage, but drinking was planned. I have zero doubt that if there was no alcohol at this party, I would have never been assaulted. At least not that night as in America, females were still assaulted at ridiculously high rates. Add alcohol, testosterone and no adult supervision and most nights it is a recipe waiting for disaster.

I don't remember how I ended up standing at the bonfire alone. I had a half filled glass of warm beer in my hand as I didn't want to be the only one not drinking. I am thankful I had only a few small sips of it that night or I might not have been able to escape my attacker. It's the little things I can look back on now and be thankful for even when I tried so hard for years to pretend that night never happened.

Back at the fire I wondered where all my friends went. I knew there were a few sections of the woods where different groups of kids were hanging out. I remember standing there thinking I must look like no one likes me since I had no one to talk to. Most of the other people at the party were older than me, which made me feel even more out of place wondering if anyone even knew who I was without my friends around me.

After a few minutes of being alone, a guy that was just a grade older than me, a major athlete and one of the "cool guys," came over to talk to me. I was so nervous...like what if I say something that makes me look too young or sound stupid. He flashed me a few smiles and made it seem like I was the only one in the world he wanted to talk to. Then he grabbed my hand and said something like "let's go somewhere quieter." I still can't remember his exact words as I unwittingly walked away with him. But boy, I remember some of the other things he said.

The next thing I knew, after barely walking away from the bonfire, he pushed me right to the ground. Maybe he said something like "oh man, I'm sorry we fell" or maybe that is just my mind trying to remember how we got from standing to on the ground so quickly. Only he did not get up; he stayed right on top of me. I can remember how heavy he felt on me. I think

I even laughed, saying something about not being able to move underneath him. But there was nothing to joke about. The next thing I knew, he was trying to unbutton my jeans and I told him to stop and get off of me. I was so confused as I was smiling and laughing the second before everything switched to me being scared of him. As I was struggling beneath him, he leaned down close to my face and said words I will never forget.

I felt frozen. I thought we were all alone where he took me and that he was really going to rape me there on the dirt floor of the woods. Someone I thought was fun because he was popular turned into someone out of a horror movie right in front of my eyes. I turned my head away from what he was saying and noticed a group of guys, much older than him and I, hooting and cheering him on. Not one was telling him to stop. I think I even saw a few clapping. I hate the thought that I could see only a few of their faces. I knew some of them that were there, and not one of them helped me.

With seeing them so excited (remember booze and testosterone), all I could think about was if he really did this, they might decide to join in as well. I had never heard the term gang-rape before but I knew the looks and sounds coming from them reminded me of a dog waiting to be thrown a piece of steak. Seeing them somehow gave me a surge of energy (now I know that to be my flight or fight response) and I started to wriggle under him to try to roll him off me. He didn't like that.

He said more unforgettable comments as my wriggling and pushing at him got more intense. Out of nowhere his fist came crashing down into my face. Remember, he was a strong athlete...the taste of blood was heavy in my mouth and I could feel him ripping at my shirt. I still don't know how many times he hit me, but I still have my bloody, ripped shirt as a reminder. Some point after the first hit, I must have let out the most deathly sound ever as finally one or two of the guys cheering us on must have realized what was going on was not mutual. Maybe they pulled him off or yelled at him as the next thing I knew he was on his knees next to me and I was able to crawl away from him. I jumped up and ran while trying to fix my shirt and wipe the blood off my face as I just knew someone would follow me.

Shockingly though, I found a quiet place to hide hoping my friends would show up so we could leave. But what happened next is something I still can't grasp to this day. One of them brought the guy that had just assaulted me over to me and told me that they heard some crap happened and wanted us to work it out so no one got in trouble. *"Are you kidding me right now! This wasn't seriously happening,"* is all I could think of! I was forced to listen to him to explain or apologize to me. I honestly still don't know what he said. All I know is I was scared to death of him and thought for sure he was going to try to finish what he started. Here I was just having been victimized by him, still sore and bleeding, and I was being treated like I was just as guilty.

I don't remember him leaving. I don't remember the ride home. All I remember is going as quietly as possible into my house to not wake my parents. I took off my bloody jacket and ripped, bloodstained shirt and hid them in case I needed proof of what happened. I washed my face, then went to bed hoping it was all a bad dream. Unfortunately, it wasn't, and the humiliation of that night was not over.

I woke up the next day, with a bloodier fat lip. However, I either hid it well, avoided my family enough, or gave some lame excuse for it, as no one questioned what happened. I laid low that day and hoped so badly that by the time school came the next day, my face would look normal. Although I wanted to call in sick to school, I didn't, but oh how I wish I would have. Once class started, a kid I had never talked to came over to me and asked me if I was ok. I was like yep, just doing homework. And he was like, no from this weekend, are you ok and why didn't you call the cops? Every ounce of my bravado crumbled. I had no idea people were talking about what happened and why a kid I had never talked to before would ask me about contacting the police. What happened to me was embarrassing, but at that point I never considered it a crime, especially as I blamed myself for so many things like partying, hanging out with older kids, and not watching where my friends disappeared to.

The kid said he was neighbors with my attacker and that one of the older guys that had been watching called him and told him to let him know if the cops came. I still wonder if the guy was hopeful I called the cops so the attacker got punished, or if he was worried if the cops came they would ask who was a witness and he wanted to hide from it. Of course I am sure it was the latter, but man how I wish he would have worried about me so much when it was happening that he would have intervened before things got so violent.

Somehow, I made it through that horrible day at school after the party. My face still hurt and I kept my eyes averted all day in hopes no one else would ask me questions or, even worse, that I would see my attacker in the hallways. I was happy when I made it home and thought I could again pretend that nothing happened. Instead, I was greeted with my parents telling me they had to talk to me.

I didn't even connect the dots that what they wanted to talk about was my assault. Without texting or social media back then my parents were pretty isolated from school or community issues. How in the world did they know? I was more confused that they would find out while I was at school then not notice my swollen face. And then they dropped a big bomb on me. Two of my friends, friends that I am pretty sure weren't even at the party, had heard about my assault and instead of checking to see how I was doing, told their parents. Their parents, who had never probably spoken even two words to my parents before, came over and told them what happened to me.

My parents were awesome, trusting and loving, however, this crushed them, especially my dad. It seems my friends' parents must not have made it sound like "your young daughter got attacked this weekend by an older guy and we wanted to make sure she was ok," but more like "do you know Jackie was out partying with boys this weekend?" Yet another blow in this awful night that just would not go away.

After a few months, I felt like I pretty much moved past the shame and the anger but really that was just a mask. I didn't trust boys and wouldn't date anyone from my school as I wasn't sure if any of them were standing around me that night watching my assault and not helping me. I even had to see my attacker for two more years of high school, where he would literally walk past me like I was just any other kid in the hall. His actions impacted my dating life and relationships for decades afterwards. I didn't trust easily, then when I did and that trust was broken, it brought me back to feeling unworthy and "less than" just because someone thought I deserved to be assaulted.

The guy and his decisions weren't worth all those years of me feeling embarrassed and inadequate. He even tried disrespecting me further years later when not once, but twice, tried to reach out to me. I didn't respond as he wasn't worth it. It was almost laughable to think he thought I cared to hear from him. Unfortunately, those that mistreat others tend to be a bit narcissistic. I was not about to feed his ego by responding.

Now I work with others that have been victimized as well as those that commit crimes. I have a unique perspective working with others, and it has helped me grow and heal. No one ever deserves to be violated by another person. There is no excuse, no amount of alcohol or any amount of sexual tension that is a reason to assault someone. If you have been victimized, please know you are worthy and deserve to heal as quickly as possible so it doesn't yank your future happiness away. You aren't alone and you deserve an abundant amount of joy and peace in your life. Find an awesome therapist, support group or positive circle of people to feel the hope that is there to safely trust other people in the future and not feel the slightest thought that any of it was your fault.

I thrive now by knowing the value I bring to this world. Every person that I can help prevent from getting assaulted through the work I do pushes my assailant further and further away from me. My guess is that I am far from the only person he hurt. I used to think maybe I could have protected others from him if I had gone to the police, yet I know that his crimes are not my cross to bear. Today, I assist other victims to address those that harmed them so they can have a voice in the criminal justice process, but only if they are ready. All of our journeys are different and there is no specific timeline on when or how we heal from something as intense as someone violating us. Maybe if I had the support I needed back then, it wouldn't have taken so long to move past the hurt. I am a totally different person today than I was back then. Even if it feels like you can't heal, I promise it gets better.

Yes, I am a victim of assault, but I am also a Social Worker, Mediator, Business Owner, Mother, Advocate, Friend, Consultant, Trainer and Executive Director. We are all so much more than one evil thing we experienced in our lives. I am excited to see how others that have been assaulted can heal, thrive and go out and conquer the world once they are ready to as well. And then, I will be even more excited to see no one ever being assaulted again.

Jackie Hallberg, LMSW is a Licensed Social Worker in the State of Michigan. She runs a nonprofit that focuses on reducing crime and conflict. She also owns two businesses helping others throughout the world. She provides training and consultation services in the areas of victim offender mediation, reentry and restorative justice practices through HOME Reentry Services. To balance out the tough work she does, Jackie also helps women feel safer traveling and organizes traveling groups through Tripping With Jax. Jackie has written a chapter in a previous anthology, "Divorce: Hard Lessons Learned" and is currently working on publishing her first travel book.

Jackie is dedicating this chapter to her mother Shirley as her mom encouraged her love of reading at a young age and has supported her through all of life's interesting turns.

The Gray Matter that Thrives Through Scarred Tissue

By Jessica Harvey

My belief is that all of our souls' journeys throughout life on earth are extremely complicated and unique, based on the obstacles we are physically, mentally, and spiritually able to handle as individuals. Though it's an easier way for populations to be analyzed, I don't necessarily agree with the standard of putting people into boxes. When reminiscing over my own life, it's difficult to know where to start my story, though experiencing left temporal lobectomy at age 17 and learning that I had been unknowingly living with a benign brain tumor for all or most of my life is when everything changed. One would think this would be an exciting, positive transformation, which is what I expected going into the surgery and how those in my life responded after the procedure. However, the side effects I was informed of by my neurological team at Children's Hospital of Philadelphia ("CHOP") before agreeing to put my head under the knife were far less severe than the actual outcome I would encounter from then onwards.

Growing up, I considered myself a very lucky child in many ways. Despite my epilepsy, specifically complex partial seizures that tended to occur in clusters, no children at my school made fun of me (or I failed to notice). In fact, after becoming close friends with some students in second grade, they would tell me what happened during my seizures, and we would enjoy laughing together about the stories. Many of my fellow schoolchildren, including those I wasn't close with, attended my father's funeral and watched me sing Amazing Grace at age 11, and in our eighth-grade yearbook I was voted both best voice and most likely to become a rocket scientist (due to my strong quantitative skills). But there also was a dark side to my childhood.

I knew internally I was mentally older than many children my age, but wasn't sure why I appeared to think differently than they did. Although I enjoyed the company of others, spending time alone to take walks in the woods and think was equally important in my life. I rarely found myself bored, and would enjoy calculating combinations and permutations on my fingers years before learning them. I would study crowds to attempt to figure out how genetics worked, write songs about helping those in need, and draw complex mazes. I enjoyed the responsibilities of getting my younger siblings ready for school each morning, as well, in replacement of my father. I felt confident that even if I didn't end up experiencing the best childhood, I had future success as an adult waiting ahead.

But, to be honest about my father's passing, I felt relief more than anything. Friends and extended family viewed him as a funny, entertaining person to be around, which was true. Yet, there was another side of him only those closest to him had to experience, involving alcohol abuse, anger, and aggression. At around the same time as his passing, my neurologist said it was appropriate to wean me off my anti-seizure medication, after being seizure-free for a year. I didn't expect that a couple months later I would experience an uncomfortable moment with a family friend, but believed that the incident would only cause my mother more pain. Given the man would visit the grave often "to converse with my father," I believed I didn't need to bring anyone else into the one-time event. Perhaps that's partially to blame for never being seizure-free again after returning to medications.

As I entered high school (where I only formerly knew five students), I became less social as I began to more keenly notice my differences in personality compared to the norm, and felt most comfortable having conversations with smaller groups or one-on-ones. I was never part of any particular clique, so when waiting for assemblies to start, I preferred to hide in the nearby bathroom instead of standing in a group where I felt I wasn't wanted. My schoolmates meant well, but some former friends would say that, in terms of me thinking more literally than most, I was "so far down at the bottom of the box that I would never think outside of it." Reflecting back, I wonder which box this was, given I felt dissimilar to most people in terms of our thinking concepts, and instead believe that difference gave me true freedom of thought and expression. Today that box might be neurodivergence.

When college-planning, my mother didn't want me leaving the house still having seizures. I started listening to the professionals at CHOP suggest I consider neurosurgery, as many medications had failed to work 100%. I was the only one aware that I was independently taking public transportation around to see movies by myself, and no strangers even noticed when I once had a seizure alone. However, I still feared revealing that fact at the time, perhaps because that would take some of my life away from me. Instead, the medical field sounded confident about the procedure. All of the neuropsychological tests sounded promising, and I felt strangely excited about this particular Wada test I'd be undergoing, which would turn off each hemisphere of my brain separately to test my memory. The day of that examination was the only day of high school I missed.

As the surgery approached, in between my junior and senior years, I started to question if I was making the right decision. Nevertheless, I had a much stronger belief in logic and proofs than intuition, and so I chose to rationally trust what the medical professionals shared. They mentioned potential side effects, such as blind spots, migraines, etc., but nothing that sounded seriously or chronically damaging. I wonder to this day if their advice would have been different if they foreknew the outcome of the existence of a benign tumor behind the scarred tissue (which increased since the surgery) they were aiming to remove.

Immediately following the recovery from physical pain, I noticed (as well as other relatives) that my personality had changed. My uncle congratulated me on "appearing normal," which I took internal offense to, as I had never wanted to be wired in the way most people appeared and had secretly taken pride in my uniqueness. The change that impacted me most was severe depression, which I had to hide because: everyone was happy for me; my mother didn't believe in such disorders; and neurology at the time considered psychiatry a pseudoscience (even when aware that the temporal lobe controls emotion through the amygdala). As I discovered this was the first true disability I was experiencing, and that it wasn't accepted as one to many people, I realized life was about to become a lot harder to endure.

One thing that did take a while to change, though, was my view of logic. When in college, I attempted to seek medical help through therapists and psychiatrists. Therapists unfortunately blamed my issues on my drinking (only on the weekends for college parties, which I hadn't done in high school) instead of recognizing that my drinking was in response to my depression and missing my previous self, rather than the other way around. Psychiatrists, meanwhile, probably didn't want to be involved in medicating me due to my complex history and the number of Americans who sue when something goes wrong. I saw their perspectives as logical and wasn't offended, so I continued to distract myself as best as I could. For some reason, I never thought that any of this experience was at the level of trauma until many years later when it was finally treated.

I survived college due to my close group of friends that really took shape at the beginning of sophomore year, and by a miracle. After giving up alcohol for Lent sophomore year, I only had a bit to drink at a party we went to early Easter morning before my boyfriend started screaming at me. I went home alone, and received a phone call from his taxi driver using his cell phone, so I paid for it to come to my dormitory and sent him a Facebook message informing him. Then I decided to drink from the bottle of mixed alcohol I had taken from my family's place. I don't remember taking over-the-counter painkillers, but found them when I woke up on the floor with vomit on my face and pills all over the place.

I saw my friend who lived in the same dorm standing over me, telling me that I needed to get up to my elevated bed unless I wanted to be removed from on-campus housing. I started telling her how I couldn't, how painful it was, but somehow I eventually was able to get up the ladder and land on my stomach. I texted her the next day, thanking her for being there for me, but she said she had stayed over her then-boyfriend's place. I was too sick all day to think about what had actually happened, and the next week my boyfriend slapping me in the face trumped what was going through my mind. It wouldn't be for another two years, around the time of our graduation in 2011, that I would remember what occurred.

By senior year, my drinking and depression had worsened, though I continued getting decent grades and interning fulltime with my friend who I thought had saved me and was then living with. The drinking was definitely a mutual flaw among many of my friends, though we also had the commonality of being smart enough to still do well academically. But with this friend in particular, it started to become a problem for her a couple months after we met as freshmen, during summer break, when her grandmother, who raised her and wasn't much older than my mother, died. We became close when she called me crying, telling me everything that had happened, but I of course wasn't able to fix the tragedy. Once we lived together, we were both going through some new sad, painful experiences that worsened our depression/trauma, and together distracted ourselves at bars and parties.

At the point when spring semester started, I was so depressed that, after drinking, I fell asleep in the snow. I did go to some AA meetings, but their stories were so much more drastic than mine, that I told myself I was fine. Meanwhile, one of the girls in our friend group randomly decided to scream at my roommate and then avoid her for months. After spring break, our whole group of friends was beginning to fall apart. I thankfully spent mine working a few days then visiting family, but all three groups who traveled came back hating one of their attendees. It wasn't until then that the friend who had ranted at my roommate came crawling back. Many people's stress and issues come out on other people, but I realized that mine came out almost always as growing self-hatred.

About a month before graduation, my still-boyfriend stopped over and, based on my clear depression, broke up with me by telling me to "figure myself out." Surprisingly to me, it actually was starting to work. It wasn't immediate, but over the next couple weeks I began realizing everything that had gotten me to where I was. And suddenly I was able to love myself once again. After that, I worked with my friends to get them to move past whatever drama had occurred for the time we had left together, including senior week tickets to the same events. And with other friends, as smart phones were becoming increasingly popular, I reminded them of the importance of living in the moment.

Once I had helped them work out their issues, I felt bored and wondered what to do next. I remembered that the summer before, I had discovered one of the few secrets I still had to myself – the memory of when I was 10 and woke up in the middle of the night having what I thought were pleasant seizures that I was able to control myself into and out of – suddenly seemed to have been an experience of speaking in tongues (which I now view as astral projection or light language). I was mildly high from cannabis in my room and jokingly asked God or a higher power, if there were to actually be an apocalypse the next year in 2012, whether I could have a role in saving people from whatever were to happen. After that, things around me started to become intensely strange.

I can't remember the order of "signs" I started to see and experience, though I recall being able to walk ridiculously fast and having a number of people stare at me as though they didn't know what they were looking at. I was starting to have great conversations with strangers, such as an older man at Foxwoods Casino, who was mesmerized at my response to his rhetorical question regarding why so many younger people had to be all dressed up for gambling, as I was walking from where one friend was to another. Our conversation ended with him telling me that I had given him a lot more hope in my generation.

I started to become more fearful when my family members and friends arrived for my graduation, in a huge mansion outside of Boston that was then inexpensive to rent. Unlike strangers, who enjoyed my new self, my family strangely did not. My siblings refused to speak to me based on whatever philosophy I was discussing, and my mom simply rolled her eyes and said I didn't look healthy after losing a significant amount of weight since they last saw me. I stayed for a while, although many people were drunk when I showed up late, then returned to Boston.

The next day, Friday, was my graduation from the business school, Saturday was my planned graduation party at the mansion, and Sunday was the university-wide ceremony. Because our School of Management, or SMG, was also jokingly an abbreviation for "sex, money, greed," I decided to do up my

139

hair and wear a green dress and gold sandals on Friday. After the ceremony and taking photos, I took a ferry with my mom and aunt to return to the suburbs to have dinner out with everyone. On the boat, we met a woman who had attended the graduation and used to work with my father. That was when I started getting chills.

Before going to dinner, my aunt noticed that one of my dress straps had strangely broken with no visible tears and used a safety pin to fix it. At the restaurant, I was anxious about returning to Boston since my friend group was meeting up that night at my friend's apartment, and I had an instinctive (and correct) feeling it would be the last time that all of us would be together. I appreciated anyone who had traveled to see me, but suddenly became more alarmed by the manner in which my uncle said to me, "it's not the end of the world." Obviously I knew it as an expression, but he seemed to mean it in a different context, and I just looked into his eyes seriously and startled, not knowing what to say. Thankfully, without question, my paternal grandparents drove me back up to Boston to see my friend drunkenly saying, "Wooh! It's the end of the world!"

When my friends then decided to split up, I chose to go with my ex-boyfriend and our guy friends to a calm rooftop party. I was processing a lot, and talking to a girl I met who had earlier noticed me at the ceremony, while noticing myself that a huge pointed-looking amount of fog was quickly entering the city from the ocean. As we left, a friend with possible autism went chasing after it, my ex ran away from us, and our other friend knew that I was well enough to get myself home. I noticed on the walk that my other dress strap had mysteriously broken.

As I returned home, I immediately looked up news about an apocalypse I had not heard of that was supposed to occur at the exact time of my graduation party. I returned back to the suburbs earlier in the day, as the fog intensified and even scared my most atheist friend and her mother on their drive. As the time got closer, I prayed for God to delay it, and all was fine. The following day, after the general ceremony, a couple of friends including her came over again. This time, she asked our group of four if anyone else was feeling the sense of a weird energy, and our other friend shivered. I finally could confirm that this wasn't just in my head, and realized that, given the number of 30th birthday parties the group of us had encountered had become an inside joke, that age was probably when the "apocalypse" would return.

And so it was, at the end of 2019 with Covid-19. My "golden year" of 31 years old was when the pandemic became serious in the US, and I immediately started to volunteer to get food to those in poverty through outdoor markets in NYC. I also joined the BLM protests from the starting weekend, and have volunteered with autistic children in Tanzania since then. Additionally, my psychiatrist had severe brain fog after catching Covid, and finally decided to take the risk of prescribing me antidepressants as I had long needed. Though circumstances have certainly not been generally thought of as going uphill since then, through darkness (perhaps at the bottom of a protective box) often shines the light we need to finally realize what we're meant to do. I interpret the dress occurrence to indicate that I may not be wealthy (as my name means in Hebrew) in terms of money, but in terms of what difference I can make for others.

Jessica is an ESG-focused Finance professional, committed to making our world more sustainable by helping a large corporate and investment bank calibrate interim industry portfolio-based greenhouse gas emission intensity reduction targets for their financing, evaluating in-scope clients quantitatively and quantitatively based on her team's climate transition framework, and working with Bankers to assist clients with their goals to reduce their carbon footprint.

She is a proudly neurodivergent, epileptic brain tumor and sepsis (followed by months of neuroinflammation) survivor, dedicated to helping others struggling with cognitive, neurological, and/or mental health conditions, particularly those from more vulnerable backgrounds than herself, through her employee resource group role at work, her college student mentoring role, her involvement on nonprofit associate boards, her connections to international impoverished villages after volunteering with special needs children in Africa, and everyday interactions.

Along with my supportive friends, I have mainly those I assist voluntarily to thank for my becoming the entity driven by helping the vulnerable I am today. The more I support others, the more rewarding my life becomes, and I believe that this is true for everyone. This photo is of me volunteering in Arusha, Tanzania, teaching and playing with primary school children with autism. I also would like to thank the people I randomly meet in New York City, from those experiencing homelessness to strangers with epilepsy I encounter at restaurants, to thank for their wise words and/or the returned help I could offer them. Without these individuals, I would not be whole. For those who would like to connect with me, I can be reached at linkedin.com/in/jessica-lee-harvey.

Overcoming Fear & Life Challenges

By: Russ Hedge

Navigating life's unwelcome surprises and thriving amidst adversity hinges on mindset and perspective. Embracing the belief that, with divine support, overcoming obstacles is possible, I've journeyed through life armed with faith and determination. Inspired by Philippians 4:13, *"I can do all things through Him who gives me strength,"* my path has been one of confronting fears, embracing choices, and persistently moving forward. Robert Frost's "The Road Not Taken" echoes my philosophy of unique paths and choices. Despite challenges, including health scares and personal battles, I've learned the value of a positive outlook, the importance of community, and the power of making each day count. Life is about choices, facing fears, and the continuous pursuit of purpose, underscored by the conviction that with intentionality and courage, we can achieve greatness. Jeanette Coron says, "Don't let your fear of failure keep you away from your destiny."

I believe God created me to do something amazing, and I get to choose my path each day.
"The Road, Not Taken," by Robert Frost, describes it well.

"Two roads diverged in a yellow wood,
And sorry I could not travel both
And be one traveler, long I stood
And looked down one as far as I could
To where it bent in the undergrowth;

Then took the other, as just as fair,
And having perhaps the better claim,
Because it was grassy and wanted wear;
Though as for that the passing there

Had worn them really about the same,

And both that morning equally lay
In leaves no step had trodden black.
Oh, I kept the first for another day!
Yet knowing how way leads on to way,
I doubted if I should ever come back.

I shall be telling this with a sigh
Somewhere ages and ages hence:
Two roads diverged in a wood, and I—
I took the one less traveled by,
And that has made all the difference."

The main theme of this poem is "choices." We all choose our path. We don't have to follow others. We are unique, and our path is unique.

As I always say, ***"Life happens, and then you choose,"*** and I've had quite a journey, with many struggles, and many choices along the way, and that is where my story begins...

I'm currently within six months of my 60th birthday. I've had a blessed life, but it's definitely not always been easy. I learned early on to just continue to show up and put one foot in front of the other, no matter what is thrown at me.

I work hard to not let my fears stop me. ***"Fear kills more dreams than failure ever will."*** - Unknown. I've learned to muster up courage, with God's help, even when it's hard. ***"Courage is not the absence of fear, but rather the assessment that something else is more important than fear."*** - Franklin D. Roosevelt

I remember one of the first big experiences where I had to overcome fear and muster my courage. It happened in high school, I played football, and was at summer practice. I don't remember how it all began, but I found myself in one of those playground fights, where everyone circles around and starts cheering. The problem was, I was in the center.

Now, I'm really a lover, not a fighter, but I found myself fighting one of my teammates. He was the Alaska Boxing Champion for his age group just a few years earlier. He punched me in the face, which was more than a little startling. I was bigger than him, but he was quicker than me. Because of my size advantage, I went to my classic headlock move which my dad taught me. It definitely stopped the punches and gave me control of the situation. After having him in the headlock for a while, I was pulled off by another teammate. I left the group running, and ran about five miles, all the way home.

I was scheduled to go back to football practice that night; I didn't want to go. I remember my dad telling me, *"Son, you have to face your fears."* So back I went, and to my surprise, there were no additional problems. I faced my fears, and everything turned out ok. In fact, as time went on, I became good friends with the teammate I had fought. I learned to face my fears, and not let fear stop me from moving forward, even through challenging situations.

So what happens when you're thrust into some major life challenges? Do you just survive, or do you fight for life and thrive? It was July 9, 1983, and I had just finished my freshman year at Oregon State University. It was a sunny summer day as I worked with my Dad in his new satellite TV business. We were struggling to install a satellite dish. Frustrated with the challenges we were having, and with each other... I decided to take a break.

I drove to a nearby golf course to play nine holes and relax. To this day, I do not remember leaving the golf course and driving home. I was driving my used, but new to me, Toyota Celica that I had owned for only seven days. As I entered

Highway 99E in Canby, Oregon, I was hit by a truck going approximately 60 miles an hour, and ended up against a tree beside a church called New Life.

First responders on the scene called LifeFlight, then closed down the highway for the helicopter to land. I was extracted from my car using the jaws of life and flown to Emanuel Hospital in Portland, Oregon.

A surgical trauma team was waiting for me. I had brain trauma and swelling, a punctured lung, both lungs collapsed, broken collar bones, broken jaw, broken ribs, and third degree burns on my feet. I was messed up, but by the grace of God, I was holding on to life. I'm a fighter, and after the trauma team finished surgery, I was in the hospital for about three weeks. I lost all memory for the first two-and-a-half weeks of my stay, though honestly, it was a blessing in disguise. Through the worst part of my recovery, God took away any memory of my pain.

My amazing parents and sister were with me every step of my recovery. It was the first part of August when I was sent home. Even through the trauma to my body, I was determined to rehab and return to Oregon State University for my Sophomore year. The doctors didn't believe I could do it, yet with God's help and strength, and my resilience, I was back at OSU in the fall.

Through life struggles, I learned with God's help, we can navigate through them. We can move forward with grit and determination to make a better life. Whether it's a physical or emotional challenge, we can come out stronger on the other side.

So wherever you are... don't settle for your negative circumstances. Break out and live with a positive mindset and perspective, no matter what you are going through.

My parents have always been so amazing. They were my role models and heroes. After so much support for me growing up, their health started to fail. They had taken care of me for so many years, and now it was my turn.

After being a lifelong smoker, my dad battled lung cancer, and after a major surgery, he almost died. He had one lung almost completely removed and struggled to recover, but finally rebounded for a few years. Bur once again his health started failing and he was getting unsteady and frail.

My mama had been diagnosed with Alzheimer's and was struggling with her memory. I made the choice to step in and help. With the guidance of my beautiful wife Leah, we sold their home and moved them to a nice retirement community. Unfortunately, through many struggles, my dad only made it another five months. After constant decline, he ended up losing his battle with cancer.

I remember the last couple days of his life. Dad was already on hospice, and things were not looking good. With the prompting of my beautiful wife, I went and spent the night with my parents in their apartment. We had been using a part time caregiver, but she was out of town and things were going badly. It was such a rough night. The next day, I hired a full time caregiver and called the hospice nurse, because Dad was in a lot of pain. It was so bad, I struggled as I was losing my hero. It was almost more than I could bear. The hospice nurse arrived and gave him pain medication, and I prayed, yet it took what seemed like hours to get him settled and calm. Finally he was resting.

I remember it like it was yesterday. He called for my mama and she came and laid down next to him on their bed. They held hands and he said, "I love you Mama"... and she replied, "I love you Papa," and they fell asleep. I was exhausted and told the caregiver I had to go home and get a few hours of sleep in my own bed, but I would be back early the next morning. I left just after 11 pm, and received a call from her about two hours later. He had stopped breathing, and had gone to be with the Lord.

It was a tough last day, however, I was so thankful for the beautiful memory of my parents loving each other and ending their married journey resting together. It taught me to make lasting memories intentionally! I have a habit of looking for the positive, even in the toughest struggle. I want to Live each moment, being present and choosing to thrive, not just survive.

I spent the next couple years loving Mama. We had so many happy moments, and I chose to record several of them. We enjoyed what I called **#HappyMomentsWithMama**. We would walk, laugh, and sing, doing laps around her memory care hallway. She called it **#LapinAndLaughin**. I shared much of this journey with my community on social media. It inspired so many through the joy my mama had, even through her last couple years of life.

I enjoyed the moments and made memories that I will never forget. Mama went to be with the Lord July 18, 2022, which was my dad's birthday. She shared in his heavenly celebration!

My journey continued. It was still July, just after my mama had passed, when my beautiful wife and I noticed what we thought was a wart on the bottom of my right foot. I treated it for a few weeks, but it didn't go away, in fact it got bigger and turned black.

Leah encouraged me to call the Dermatologist. They took a good look and decided a biopsy was necessary. Within a few days it came back as an invasive Melanoma, Stage 2A Cancer, and I was referred to OHSU in Portland.

At OHSU, they found another small spot and did another biopsy, which also came back positive for Melanoma. Surgery was scheduled for Friday, November 11. They were removing a large area of my right instep, but felt they could get all of the cancer. I was also undergoing Plastic Surgery at the same time to rebuild my instep.

During the surgery they also took out one of my lymph nodes just to make sure the cancer had not spread.

The surgery went well. I spent a night at OHSU, and they sent me home the next day to begin the slow recovery process. The area removed on my foot and the lymph node were sent off to pathology for testing. We were all feeling optimistic, including the doctors.

Well, Life is full of surprises and on Thursday, November 17, I received one. The day started off well. I went to my Post-Op appointment at OHSU and was told the plastic surgery they did to repair my foot, after my Melanoma Cancer removal, was looking good and I was healing as expected.

My beautiful wife, daughter and I drove home and grabbed some Chic-fil-A on the way. I was tired, but feeling good overall. When we got home, I opened my email. I saw a MyChart message with the test results from Pathology, and was expecting to see good news. The first part was good. The bottom of my foot where they cut out the cancer looked good. The outer tissue was cancer free... Very Good News.

The next part was not so good. In the lymph node they removed from my groin area they found a tumor. In a phone call later that evening, my Oncologist Surgeon explained that the the cancer had gone from Stage 2A to Stage 3C, and further treatment was needed. They were also doing additional tests and scans to make sure it had not gone any further.

After the initial shock of the diagnosis, I felt God saying to me, "It is going to be ok. I've got this!" I believed it then, and I believe it now... God's not done with me yet!

My Oncologist was confident it was very treatable, and started things in motion. On Nov 22, I underwent a PET scan and MRI to determine if the cancer had gone any further in my body. Praise God the results came back negative and no further cancer was found.

There was a whole lot more ahead for me. Additional treatment and more surgery. I also became a Type 1 Diabetic, had digestive issues, vertigo, hearing and sight challenges, but I never stopped believing.

In fact, I shared my journey to inspire and encourage others, keeping my God-given positive perspective in spite of what I was going through. With an amazing family and wonderful friends supporting me, I am truly Blessed!

I've always chosen to live life to the fullest, be positive and encourage others, and that will not change. I will live, and I will believe the best is yet to come. I received so much support, and was so thankful for my family and friends! My online community supported me from all over the globe. My purpose is to encourage people, no matter what they're going through, I believe *"God works all things for the Good for those who love Him!"* Romans 8:28, so I continue to trust God and encourage people to stay positive and keep a good perspective.

Your perspective is up to you! With intention and courage you can do the amazing things God has created you to do. Don't let yourself get discouraged when you stumble, because that is inevitable. You are human. But, you can overcome, and with the right mindset, make things better for you and others, no matter what the circumstances.

Your circumstances do not define you!

You can thrive, not just survive!

In scripture, God says, ***"Don't be afraid, for I am with you. Don't be discouraged, for I am your God!"*** Isaiah 41:10. There is something much greater than you and I, and when you lean into that strength, the impossible becomes possible.

Your community is also an important part of your journey. We were created for community, so connect and gain strength today. Mother Teresa said, *"I alone cannot change the world, but I can cast a stone across the waters to create many ripples."* Your life affects more than you know.

No matter what you are going through, you can create ripples with your actions, and then work together with your community to achieve amazing results. These results come to fruition through collaboration. Communities working together. *"We cannot live only for ourselves. A thousand fibers connect us with our fellow men."* - Herman Melville

You are but one fiber, yet can make a positive impact when you connect to others.

There is power in numbers. We are better together, with love, compassion and a sense of community. This is a key element in creating something significant with your life, and this often happens through challenges and struggles.

I am here to encourage and inspire you to live a purpose-driven life of significance. That is what God has called me to do, and I do it with the help of my community.

Are you letting your fears and false expectations get in the way? *"People get so caught up in the fact that they have limits that they rarely exert the effort required to get close to them."* - James Clear. It takes work. We are all limited by our humanity, but we can make great things happen in spite of our challenges, if we choose to.

Now is your time to live your Best Life. Don't wait. You can find significance in life.

You can make improvements one step at a time... one percent at a time. *"Making a choice that is 1 percent better or 1 percent worse seems insignificant in the moment, but over the span of moments that make up a lifetime these choices determine the difference between who you are and who you could be. Success is the product of daily habits – not once-in-a-lifetime transformations."* - James Clear

How do you thrive instead of just surviving? The answer lies in your mindset and perspective. Choose to be a world-changer and a difference-maker. Even through the most challenging circumstances, you can do it! I have learned through my own challenges, whether it be overcoming fear, tragic accidents, or health challenges, it can be done. I have done it. There is a God who loves you, and your faith can propel you to better days ahead. Just keep on moving forward, one step at a time. You can thrive your way through!

Why not start today!

Russ Hedge is here to encourage and inspire others to live a purpose-driven life of significance, creating World Changers and Difference Makers. To encourage people to use their God-Given Gifts to do Amazing Things!

Russ is a Marketing Coach, Keynote Speaker, Livestream Producer and Internationally Best Selling Author.

He is a positive force in today's busy, hectic, and often negative business environment.

Russ loves to encourage, inspire, and make people smile. That's why he is known as an "Inspiration Specialist."

He has been married to his beautiful wife Leah for over 36 years and has 2 adult children, Kyla and Connor, and a daughter-in-law, Gabby. His goal is to add value to people by encouraging and helping them live a more engaged and positive life.

Connect with Russ at russ@russhedge.com.

The Hedge Family

I dedicate this to my Beautiful Wife Leah and my family. It is God and their support that has kept me going through it all. I thank God for Leah every day and her resilience in helping me and caring for me, even though her own physical trials she has stayed beside me every step of the way. She is a gift from God! And, to my amazing children, Kyla and Connor, and my Daughter-in-Law Gabby. So much support. Finally, to my sister Brenda who has been available any time I need help. You are all amazing!

Think Like a Winner (Live like a Winner)

By: Willie J.

In business, living in the grey can be incredibly beneficial. It encourages flexibility, fosters innovation, and builds resilience. By accepting that not all answers are in black and white, leaders can create a culture of learning and adaptability, crucial for navigating the complexities of the business world. This mindset allows for creative solutions, encourages risk-taking within reason, and supports the notion that failure is not a defeat but a stepping stone to greater success. Embracing the grey areas in decision-making can lead to unexpected opportunities and breakthroughs, reinforcing that winning begins and ends with the mindset.

After a multitude of unintentional mistakes, hard failures, and great frustrations in my life, I knew that something had to immediately transform inside of me, but I wasn't quite sure of how I was going to do it. Or how I could adequately pivot my lifestyle for more excellent wins, more significant gains, and more tremendous success as I grow forward with my life. Well, If the truth be told. It was simply because I needed more positive self-imagery, self-awareness, and self-discovery to overcome the real root of all my problems.

I clearly recall stating once before, that I would often find myself living with the subconscious belief that if I had lived a good life of morals and righteousness, everything good and excellent would automatically happen for me. Well, let me tell you something about that one.

NOT SO! Meanwhile, I started to dive a lot deeper

into my faith and relationship with God, which consisted of intense meditation, isolation, and prayer during my most trying moments, and he would soon answer me in a still but powerful voice, letting me know that.

So as a man thinketh in his heart, so is he, and you gradually become what you think about most of the time. That's right, we become what we think about each day, and with our thoughts, we create our realities.

He was letting me know that an immediate new mind shift was very necessary, and when you begin to spell this word backward, you are then left with "shift mind." Meaning, that I had to gradually reset and shift my mindset into that of a winner, and when I finally realized that most of my failures in life had resulted in the way that I had been thinking about myself over time. The whole trajectory of my lifestyle started to change drastically for the better.

Yelp, that's right, winning is a lifestyle of growth that is consistently cultivated and developed from the inside out. Now, let me say that again. Winning is a lifestyle of growth that is consistently cultivated and developed from the inside out", and when you begin to spell this word "lifestyle" backward, you are then left with "stylelife."

Very similar to a skilled beautician or a skilled barber who is styling someone's hair to have a beautiful display or a beautiful outcome. So we must style our own lives in this same manner and do this by thinking, speaking, reacting, and responding to all of life's circumstances.

Some of us call this great principle and law "The Law of Response" because the universe will always correspond to the response that it has been given. Our daily thoughts, actions, and reactions are like echoes that boomerang right back into our world.

Where Winning Begins

I truly believe that before we can understand the value of winning, we must first understand and comprehend where winning begins, and from my knowledge, wisdom, and understanding. All winning begins and ends with the mindset. It derives from one possessing a certain mindset and a series of failed attempts to become better at something, and without a doubt, everyone wants to win big, but very few people want to fail big in the beginning.

That said, we must be willing to fail to win and be honest and transparent. I didn't always handle this winning concept too well. So, I would eventually learn to think beyond the veil and against all odds of my biggest mistakes, errors, and present struggles. That's right! We must fail to win. The unique Les Brown said that "**Failure** is not a destination; it's an invitation to unforeseen victories.

My Unlimited Thinking

Once I finally learned how to think outside of the box of my external reality and above other people's expectations of me, everything began to shift for me in a very miraculous way. Discovering that there are genuinely no boundaries or no limits to what we can do, be, or have in this life, and when I discovered the epiphany that my only limits to winning in life were me and my mindset.

I began soaring like a skyrocket beyond my wildest dreams and most giant imaginations, and not even the sky's the limit, only my mind. Anything and everything is possible with God because he created us all to be unlimited beings and co-creators. We all have unlimited God-given superpowers if we could only believe that we do.

The amazing Napoleon Hill said "Whatever the mind can

conceive and believe, the mind can achieve. You have to have your CBA degree which means the ability to Conceive, Believe, and Achieve. That's right if you can conceive it, you can believe it, and if you can believe it you can achieve it.

Now, before I could ever co-author 3 #1 International Best-Selling books in less than six months, or hit the #1 spot in the LA weekly Top 10, I found myself being featured on the front cover of FORBES MOROCCO Magazine.

I had to conceive it, perceive it, and then believe it first in my mind by way of my own vision board. I was writing out my vision and making it plain enough to see in my mind's eye, and you know what? It all surely came to pass with great overflow and with great abundance.

Believe in You by Being Yourself

To my surprise, many leaders today often struggle with what we call Imposters Syndrome. It is when a person with great winning potential is found struggling with their own identity, self-insufficiency, inadequacies, and self-worth. Always feeling as if they are not good enough to succeed at being themselves.

Have you ever struggled with this? I think that we all have at some point in our lives Meanwhile, through many trials, errors, and reflection, I began to refuse to live a life filled with compromise and with filtered disguise.

I soon learned that being myself is always good enough, and I've always said that if I can't live out the fulfillment of my big dreams being my own self. Then those big dreams are not worth me living at all. See, God created us all to be unique, original, and authentic in a most amazing way, and there was no mistake in the way that he manufactured us to look, move, breathe, or achieve great things in life.

So always believe in yourself by being yourself and staying true to your identity. This is what true winners do, and please remember that when we truly believe in ourselves wholeheartedly without wavering or unbelief. We can begin living our best lives with our own brilliance and authenticity.

Brainwash Your Mind for Success

When you begin to spell this word brainwash backwards you then have "wash brain "which is another way of saying wash your brain. A mental detox cleansing is the act of getting rid of all of our negative and toxic thought patterns. For instance, if we were to just rely on washing up, taking a shower, or taking a bath once a week. We are sure to face the inevitable risk of uncleanness or the risk of having a bad odor. Neither will brushing our teeth for just one day prevent damage of your personal hygiene. Now, imagine that for a moment.

However, this is the same approach we must take when washing our brains and cleaning up our toxic thoughts for success, and I would soon learn that just as we can become brainwashed by TV, people, politics, and social media. We can also manipulate or brainwash our minds to win and succeed. Then I eventually started to comprehend that I could trick, reprogram, and shift my mindset into thinking in the direction it should be. It works like a heavenly charm.

Winning in a Time of Crisis

Without a shadow of a doubt, this life can be very shocking at times. However, this is how we learn to adapt to it and "Grow with the Flow fully." As I am finalizing this chapter right now, I am silently grieving the recent passing of my dear great aunt, whom I like to call "Aunt Lee", but at the same time, I find myself celebrating her transition along with all those precious memories that we shared.

It is all about having the right mental perspective and being willing to comprehend that she is now resting in heaven with the good Lord and kicking it with my mom and the other loved ones. R.I.P. Now ironically, a week later, I woke up to a very unexpected and most prestigious honor that I would be featured in the "New Jersey Times" Top 20 Influential Personalities To Look Out For In 2024.

Can you Imagine that? Wow, talking about having some Sunshine with the Rain. This is why I often say to myself and the world that my Pain is always Gained at the end of the day! Because I expect it to be. I was so elated and blown away with a heart of gratitude to be featured alongside some of the world's most amazing leaders and CEOs from Starbucks, Zoom, WhatsApp, Uber, and many more.

See, in this life there will always be unfortunate circumstances, struggles, and unexpected crises that are out of our control, and If there is one thing that I know, true winning comes at a great price and with great sacrifice. It can sometimes be downright difficult but well worth it in the end game.

The legendary Martin Luther King Jr. said, "Every crisis has both its dangers and its opportunities. Each can spell either salvation or doom."

In other words, we must find a way to "Leverage every moment whether it be good or bad" and know that God and the universe are always working in unison and everything out in our favor. It's all about the outlook and how we view a thing from every angle of its true existence.

Some people would call this "Mind over Matter." This is the capacity to make the conscious choice or decision to think beyond the veil of our existing problems. A mantra and a motto that I have lived by for many years now, possessing the ability to transmute all my setbacks, shortcomings, and failures into my most significant victories and comebacks.

Yea, you heard me correctly. Our setbacks are simply opportunities to have our greatest comebacks growing forward, and I can recall nearly losing everything just to gain everything back in return. My darkest story eventually became my greatest glory through God's blessings, miracles, promotions, and testimonials.

So, dear reader, always remember that the world within our minds is always far greater and larger than the world around us. Nothing Is more supreme than the God-given dreams that live deep inside of us all. You just have to believe that it's true! Which reminds me of a great quote made by the legendary "Forbes Riley" that says:

"Dream it, Believe it, and Achieve it " That's right, to win big in life we should always be ready to dream it, believe it, and achieve it in a grand fashion. Quite similar to one of my own personal mantras that I still live by today which is "Believe Big, Dream Big, and Receive Big in return." Now say that with me again "Believe Big, Dream Big, and Receive Big in return."

Ok, now why did I have you to repeat that for me? It is simply because when we say our dreams and goals out loud to ourselves by way of repetition or by way of repetitive affirmations. We begin to build up the belief system of our subconscious mind as well as build up our faith, and it is written that faith comes by hearing a thing repeatedly, so the more that we speak it out, we can begin to eventually live it out.

However, I must fully warn you: please be very aware of all the dream and vision killers that may be surrounding you. Because they will surely come to throw you off your A game, please trust and believe me, I know. They will often make vague attempts to try and diminish the quality and outcome of your biggest goals and biggest dreams. Usually because they are afraid and lack the inner courage enough to dream big for themselves. You know the saying, misery loves company.

What am I really trying to say here? Respectfully, I am saying never ever to allow anyone to minimize and ostracize the totality and value of your dreams and ambitions in life. Regardless of how they may feel about it. Do it big anyway! No friend, No foe, No family or anyone in this world is ever worth belittling your God-given talents, purpose, character, and true identity as a champion. I learned a long time ago never to try and fit in with many people and areas where you truly don't belong.

Now go relentlessly hard after that purpose-driven goal or that goal-driven purpose when you say it backwards, and always be fearless and courageous enough to put your own big dreams to the test. Don't be afraid to fail, just fail forward, make the adjustments, and do a better job the next time around. One of my greatest mentors, John C. Maxwell said that "It's one thing to have a dream. It's another to do the things needed to achieve it."

To thrive in the grey zone, a domain where ambiguity reigns and straightforward answers are elusive, we must embrace a mindset of adaptability, resilience, and proactive engagement. Immediate action, coupled with a strategic approach, paves the way for gaining meaningful traction. This traction is not merely about making incremental progress but also about attracting the right kind of attention and support from those around us and those in positions of influence. It's about crafting a legacy of success through hard work, intelligent strategies, and unwavering commitment. Let us never lose sight of the immense potential that lies within our collective efforts and dreams. As champions of our own destiny, we must persevere in our quest for greatness, bolstered by the knowledge that every challenge overcome in the grey zone adds to our mental fortitude and brilliance. Let this be a call to action for all who seek to make an undeniable mark on the world: Embrace the grey zone, leverage your unique strengths, and march forward with confidence and determination until the finish line is crossed and your dreams are realized. Remember, in the journey of leadership and success, mental resilience is not just an asset but the essence of brilliance. Like I always say "resilience is brilliance" and "never stop winning."

Willie J. a native of East Saint Louis, Illinois is the founder and CEO of the global award winning company "Pure Mission Entertainment ." He is an award winning entrepreneur, poet, recording artist, Maxwell leadership coach, speaker and International Bestselling Author who has co-authored 3 #1 International Bestsellers. He has been seen on platforms like YAHOO! FINANCE, ABC 30, CBS, GQ MAGAZINE, FORBES, BROADWAY WORLD, LA WEEKLY, NY WEEKLY, NEW JERSEY TIMES, and many more. His soulful music has garnished over 28 million streams worldwide in over 184 countries. Along with two front cover features in both the Morocco Forbes Magazine and the LA Business. Willie J. and his company are on a mission to create more hope through arts, coaching, and entertainment while empowering people, changing lives. For more info about Willie J please visit puremissionent.com or follow him on instagram: @williejpme

Once again, my company Pure Mission Entertainment is always excited about helping charitable causes and meaningful projects that can bring about more global change, impact, and awareness.

Our motto is always about creating more hope through arts and entertainment and empowering more people and changing more lives with God's help.

After the massive success of several charity-based projects that we have already done globally over the years for the Hurricane Maria victims and the victims of Covid-19 and more

We are elated to have this golden opportunity to create more change and make a huge difference with our chapter in this book for Evertreen.

 With the collaborative efforts of helping to protect and restore forests and by involving more farmers, creating more livelihoods for people living in poverty, and empowering them to become life changing agents of the forest globally.

This is simply why we do what we do, we love and support you!

Forged in Fire: A Story of Resilience and Rebirth

By: Gabe Leal, Love Enthusiast

Forget superheroes who leap from skyscrapers or conquer dragons. My greatest battleground was the bleak, monotonous expanse of the "grey zone" - a life stuck on repeat, devoid of color, where dreams faded faster than laundry in the sun. But unlike most fairytales, this wasn't about a single, epic clash. It was a thousand tiny victories, a relentless chipping away at the monotony, fueled by a flicker of defiance buried deep within. This is the story of how I dared to paint my masterpiece on the canvas of the ordinary, not with grand gestures, but with the brushstrokes of everyday choices. Prepare to be surprised because triumph, my friends, can whisper just as loudly as it roars. Now, step into the grey zone with me and see how even the faintest spark can ignite a revolution.

Before our flame can illuminate the darkness... we must summon the courage to strike a match. While sitting in the absence of light, pain was my companion. The aching in my entire body had overwhelmed me; all I wanted to do was hide. I felt like a five-year-old child afraid of the dark, hiding beneath the covers to shield myself from the fear. I couldn't control the tears and anxiety, my mind longed for my thoughts to stop and my inner voice to quit speaking. "You're a failure!" constantly being repeated.

The creaking of the windows as the wind hit the glass felt like a whisper of terror. As I found myself curled up in the fetal position, tears streaming down my face, I couldn't help but think, "How the fuck did I get here?" The voice in my head shouted louder, "What the hell is wrong with you, Gabe?" Overwhelmed and lost, thoughts of ending it all began to take hold. "How can I stop feeling?" I wondered. "Maybe death is the answer?"

It was hard to find meaning in life when everything felt so empty and meaningless. Despite having a family, and a home, it all seemed pointless. I was going to do it. What would be the easiest way with no pain? A quick slip away from escaping into nothingness. Images of my children crying because their father was no longer alive were running through my head. But living a life without purpose seemed just as cruel. I couldn't take it anymore.

This flame was more valuable to my family extinguished. "How bad could life be at this point?" Forty-four years is all I could manage—a broken man, with little to show for the years of existence in the world. I always hoped for something better, something good. My soul longed for more. Months earlier in a workplace accident, my foot was shattered with multiple fractures. This injury was the genesis of my spiral downward. The ominous clouds had formulated overhead. They were shadowing below a path into darkness.

I didn't have many things to hang on to in my mind except my ability to work, earn a living, and support my family. In one fell swoop those things changed. The injury and the aching would require surgery, therapy, and more pain. It forced me out of work for an extended period. Not only did I lose my ability to be a provider for my family, but my peace of mind vanished like a raindrop in the ocean. Life already had me walking a tightrope as the only provider for my family. Lots of mental anguish had built up like a weighted anvil that grew heavier by the day.

Financial pressures intensified as the children's needs grew and the bank account dwindled. How was I going to keep the roof over our heads? Where were our next meals going to come from? How was I going to keep us from drowning? The pressure had cracked me and stripped me of every ounce of will to continue. My vessel felt barren, void of meaning, numb to the aching emptiness that gnawed at my very core.

Little did I know how this would compound the stressors that intensified an already hectic life. The thoughts entering my mind all led me to want to extinguish my flame. It was a different mindset from the familiar, drawn-out doldrums of everyday living. Darkness called me, whispering sounds so soothing, like the crashing waves that splashed ashore on the sands. An inexplicable pull resonated within me, drawing me closer to the cool embrace of the ocean. This scared the shit out of me, but I couldn't stop myself from thinking about it. The tears were flowing uncontrollably, and the only thing I could do was pull the cover over my head while I lay curled on the couch.

Next to me was the bottle of OxyContin prescribed for my pain. Tightly gripped in my hand the thought of twisting the cap and swallowing every pill was the only thing that could comfort me in the moment. If I downed this whole bottle, I would fall asleep and the world would fade to black. No goodbyes, no explanations, just punching out from life.

The tears subsided for a brief moment, I looked up and asked God to help me. "Please, if you still love me send me a sign that you are listening." My hands trembled with the bottle in one hand and the other on my heart. Lying there just as broken as a pane of glass in shattered pieces, I wept. What was I waiting for? A sign, anything that would deter me from opening that bottle.

Suddenly there was a calmness that laid upon me, like a warm blanket on a cold day. Stillness in a moment of chaotic energy. I felt something vibrate, the tremble of my phone. It did it again, and this time I recognized the feeling. Searching for the sensation as it vibrated again, I gripped it in my hand as I put down the bottle momentarily. Turning the phone over and taking a glance, I saw one message.

Debating on whether to open the message or the bottle, I prayed this was the sign. It was a message from my dear friend Kate. We had been friends for a while, as we both had our struggles and leaned on each other for support. I hadn't heard from her for some time.

It was a simple message but one that would change my life forever. It was a video from actor Matthew McConaughey titled "This Is Why You're Not Happy | One of The Most Eye-Opening Speeches." I didn't hesitate to open it. This moment of calmness laid over me and as the message began, every sound, every word, every beat of the music penetrated me. The message played and his voice was the most peaceful siren that I could imagine. With every word, I felt a warmth inside me burning with momentum.

They say that alcoholics have this "aha" moment that comes as a moment of clarity, a moment when through the haze of alcohol and the deeply ingrained denial a clear thought appears where they want to stop using and desperately find a way to get sober. It's the closest way I can describe what happened to me. As the message played, there was this prodigious touch on my soul and I understood this was my path.

The words that were uttered resonated with stepping stones to make a shift in my life. The tears stopped briefly but as they began again, they had a different feeling, as though these were tears of joy. "Was this God?" It had to be. I have never felt anything like that before or since, and it was only for a moment. It felt like I was in the presence of something unexplainable, and honestly, I didn't need an explanation. It was peace. It was harmony. It was clarity.

The next day I awoke with a different feeling...I knew two things for sure. I was alive and I could decide to change my life. Yesterday I welcomed death, today I invited life. There were no plans, no roadmap, and no idea what I needed to do. All that concerned me was to do anything different. Even with the pain in my foot, I was determined to push myself. Life had to move forward or fall back into darkness.

I played the video over and over again. Each time, I discovered something new, something different. I began watching more motivational videos, and looked for different outlets to find resources, these things became agents of change for me. I began reading books and listening to audio conversations. My mission was to search high and low to find the one thing that spoke to me, something that sparked my creativity. I struggled with trying to write books and blogging, but nothing was quite speaking to me. Then I found my sparkle moment while watching YouTube. Live video....the concept was foreign to me but it stuck out like a sore thumb.

I needed to find a formula that I could use over and over again to spur my quest to learn and grow, something that could facilitate development and be sustainable. This was going to challenge my psyche because since fourth grade I had a fear of any kind of public speaking. "How the hell was I going to get on camera and talk?" I couldn't even find the courage to speak up over the top of all my coworkers, how was I going to do this for strangers?

Determination was the only thing I would accept; giving up was not an option. I searched high and low on the internet to learn more about live streaming. I found a mentor online and with his guidance, he led me to the position I presently sit in. His name is Russ Johns, and his openness and kindness in giving an unknown individual like me his time and wisdom showed me that people do have compassion for others. This would become a model for me. As frightening as it was for me to speak in public, talking in front of a camera wasn't any easier. Ready to face my fear head-on, I purchased a webcam from Amazon. I set it up on a white bedsheet, a folding table, and my laptop in my garage. On February 19, 2020, the camera turned on, the lights (as bad as they were) shined, a Lavalier microphone was pinned to my shirt, and after a ton of nerves, I went live for the first time. This was the first step in learning so much about myself.

The goal was simple, share stories of incredible people who have overcome their struggles, broken the shackles of despair, and radiated their energy to change the world around them. The beginning was tough because of my inexperience, but it was also the best part of the failures. I learned something new about myself with each interview. With each story of resiliency, I received a jolt of energy to push forward. Each conversation was a small victory. Every word spoken became a milestone in my rebirth.

In the process, my life turned upside down, because once you become an agent of change, the life you once led is no longer the one you choose. In this moment you begin to discover a power inside. The hard part of changing anything is letting go of the fear. I feared facing my life as I had constructed it, and almost chose the path of suicide to find escape. I was willing to lose it all, my family, my kids, my health all because of the pressure of failure as a husband, a father, and as a provider. Deep down inside, it was God who was molding me to be ready, to have all my walls down, and be prepared to accept the plan he had intended for me all along.

The winds of change were already in motion. Once they blow you into the direction you're meant to follow, you have to let go of the things that can't carry any longer. I lost friends, my spouse, and everything that was once comforting. I also realized I had a lot to gain.

My message to everyone reading my story is this, despite

the darkness we sometimes find ourselves in, we can fight – if we don't give up, we can make it one more day and there is light at the end of the tunnel. There is hope above all. Our struggles are the things that shape us. There are lessons we can take from failing even in the direst of moments. I've spent the last four years learning to accept my flaws and being okay with who I am now.

After I created over five hundred show episodes, there are now thousands of hours of interviews and conversations with amazing people. Each one is unique, each leaving an imprint on my soul. Fueled by curiosity, one question was crafted that I would ask all my guests: "When the book is said and done on your story, what kind of legacy do you want to leave behind, what do you want to be remembered for?" This had special implications because it remained one of my unanswered questions. Sitting here writing this now, my gut tells me I have the answer that I sought. I want to leave a legacy of love and empathy for the world to see and feel. I want to be remembered as a man who lived every day to the fullest extent and did it with kindness and compassion for all those who crossed my path.

My lived purpose is simple, help ignite the flames of all that seek light, to be a conduit to help others find their voice, purpose, and meaning in this life. What I have forged through the scolding embers of my journey serves me in using these amazing gifts to craft stories, and share experiences that unite people together. Going through the fire gave me many burn scars that I wear proudly as a constant reminder of how far I've come from living amid the grey zone.

While the path may be forged in fire, remember that the

flames can forge incredible strength and resilience within you. Embrace the lessons learned from hardship, for they become the stepping stones that propel you beyond the grey zone. Stepping out of the comfort of neutrality allows you to chase your aspirations with newfound passion and purpose. Embrace the vibrant life that awaits beyond the flames, knowing that within you lies the unyielding spirit that carried you through the fire.

What is a "Love Enthusiast"? That's me, Gabe! As an individual, I identify as a "love enthusiast". This means I have a strong interest and passion for various aspects of love. I deeply appreciate love in all its forms, including romantic love, friendship, familial love, and self-love. I enjoy exploring these emotions in different contexts, such as literature, history, or psychology.

I want to give special thanks to my best friend and partner in love Yvette Richardson. You're the flame that fans this man's fire. My children Leonor (Brat), Sophia, Cordelia, Joaquin, Bonita, and my new family members Skylar, Cheyenne, and Naomi. They inspired me to excel as an example and to follow my heart. My best friend Dayna Fellows for the best support a guy can ask for. And one last special dedication to my dear friend, best-selling novelist and, by the Grace of God, savoir Kate Stewart, (I finally leaped)!

The Nap that Introduced Me to My True Self

By: Jacquellene Lukich

In the tapestry of my life, a defining thread weaves through a remarkable tale of resilience and rebirth. A chapter that began with the sudden rupture of a brain aneurysm, plunging me into a profound 21-day coma. Amidst the shadows of uncertainty, the guiding hand of a visionary neurosurgeon emerged, wielding unconventional techniques that became a beacon of hope. This courageous, bold healer pioneered a medical intervention that defied the odds and reshaped the landscape of aneurysm treatment. The defining moment in my life intertwines through unwavering determination and perseverance. It all began with an unexpected challenge, plunging me into a profound period of adversity.

Emerging from the cocoon of unconsciousness and the depths of hardship, I embraced a renewed lease on life. I embraced a newfound resilience, transcending the limits of adversity. A testament to the human spirit's indomitable strength, I emerged not just as a survivor but as one who thrived. A decade on, I stand as a living testament to the extraordinary fusion of medical innovation and personal tenacity.

Unified with my loving family and steadfast support system, I navigated the complexities of healing, embarking on a journey where physical, mental, and spiritual realms converged. As I thrive in the vibrant mosaic of life, I find purpose in illuminating the path and guiding others along their journey of resilience as a living testament to the transformative power of perseverance, innovation, and the unyielding human spirit.

In the woven threads of my life before the profound

twist of fate, I navigated a landscape filled with triumphs and tribulations. A high achiever in all endeavors, my journey was underscored by an unwavering commitment to integrity and familial responsibility. Yet, amidst the peaks of success, I grappled with the shadows cast by the disintegration of a once-promising marriage.

As the sole provider for my two beautiful daughters, I faced the challenging reality of a disappearing father, a man who evaded not only familial responsibilities but the echoes of his own existence. My European heritage gave me a family steeped in strength, support, and unyielding opinions. Their presence became the bedrock upon which I forged ahead, weathering the storm of a divorce that threatened to tarnish the very fabric of our esteemed reputation.

The divorce proceedings were not merely legal intricacies but tumultuous journey through emotional turbulence. A failed marriage, a shattered union, and the looming prospect of being the harbinger of perceived shame to my esteemed family weighed heavily on my shoulders. The commitment to shield my daughters from the emotional fallout became my Promise and goal. I stood resolute, my focus unwavering on their well-being, even as the tempest of divorce raged.

In the face of adversity, I chose the path of fairness and equity, refraining from the siren call of bitterness and greed. My aspirations were modest yet profound – a shared financial split, a fair separation that reflected the dissolution of a union and a commitment to preserving the sanctity of familial bonds. Supported by my close-knit circle of friends and the solid presence of my family, I endeavored to navigate the complex terrain of divorce with grace and grit.

Throughout this turbulent chapter, I remained a paragon of resilience, driven by the unshakeable spirit to uphold the values that defined me. My commitment to doing the right thing, coupled with the fortitude of my family and the unwavering support of dear friends, became the crucible in which I forged a path toward healing. The storm clouds gathered, but within this crucible, I discovered a strength that would later prove instrumental in facing an even more formidable challenge in the unseen chapters of my life.

In the intricate tapestry of my life, the chapters that unfolded before the onset of the life-altering brain aneurysm were marked by a strong spirit, complex family dynamics, and a commitment to navigating the storm of divorce. As a high achiever in all facets of life, I was thrust into the unfamiliar territory of divorce court while simultaneously ascending the corporate ladder to provide financial stability for my two daughters. The burden of being the sole provider weighed heavily on my shoulders.

My European family, renowned for their strength and firm opinions, provided an anchor of support amidst the treacherous divorce proceedings. The dissolution of my marriage carried not only personal implications but a societal weight as I contended with the fear of tarnishing my family's reputation. Yet, guided by a commitment to integrity and fairness, I sought a divorce that was not marred by greed but aimed for an equitable split to safeguard my children from emotional trauma.

The onset of the aneurysm was an unforeseen cataclysm, disrupting the already challenging narrative of my life. Balancing the complexities of divorce court and the corporate climb, I faced an invisible adversary that would test my strength to my core. Deprived of warning signs, the aneurysm struck abruptly, turning a routine Black Friday shopping excursion into a life-threatening ordeal.

My collapse perplexed my daughters, initially dismissed as dehydration. However, a perceptive paramedic recognized the gravity of the situation and administered life-saving measures. The journey from one hospital to another was a desperate race against time, with my sister receiving ominous messages, preparing her for the worst. In the pivotal moments at the second hospital, an Angel in the form of a doctor, sent by Divine intervention, stood ready to tackle the precariousness of my existence.

The impact of my near-fatal experience reverberated far beyond the hospital walls, sending shockwaves through my entire network of family and friends across the globe. The collective prayers, untiring support, and Divine intervention that orchestrated the presence of skilled medical professionals shaped the narrative of my survival. My recovery became a testament not only to medical advancements but also to the resilience fostered through the turbulent journey of divorce and corporate pursuits.

In the wake of this life-altering event, the fragility of existence became palpable, and the tapestry of my life took on new hues. The strength of familial bonds, the power of prayer, and the interconnectedness of a global network of well-wishers became enduring themes in the following chapters, defining a narrative of survival, resilience, and the profound impact of one woman's journey in a world that rallied around her.

In the cocoon of a 21-day coma, I embarked on a profound journey, a suspended state of existence that served as both respite and renewal. It was a much-needed reprieve from the fierce narrative of my life, a sanctuary where my body could heal and recoup, preparing for a second chance at a brighter, more vibrant existence.

The vivid tapestry of my coma unfolded in two distinct realms. In one, I found myself amidst paradisiacal landscapes — a masterpiece I've never seen before of serene beauty, with vibrant flowers, lush green foliage, and tranquil waterfalls. It was a sanctuary of peace, an oasis where the scars of life began to fade, and tranquility enveloped me in it's comforting embrace.

Yet, another realm revealed itself, a series of all-white hallways and grand doors. In the ethereal company of beings emanating warmth and love, their forms obscured by radiant light, I walked in a space where energy infused me with a sense of safety and protection. A library adorned the path, with shelves upon shelves of stunning white leather and gold-bound books, a bibliophile's dream. The beings informed me that I had already traversed the contents of these volumes, an intriguing revelation that left me yearning for more time among the literary treasures.

Simultaneously, as I navigated these realms of serene landscapes and celestial hallways, my family and friends stood anchored in a world of uncertainty. The pivotal surgical intervention, an unprecedented procedure undertaken by a skilled Doctor, held their collective breath. Nights turned into days in the waiting room, my mother and sister never leaving my side. My sister and doctor became the orchestrators of crucial decision-making and navigated uncharted territory with unwavering trust.

The medical staff, inspired by my Doctor's reputation and my sister's grace, went above and beyond, investing in my recovery and a vision of a reborn future. Their collective efforts transcended the call of duty, prayers echoing through hospital corridors, resonating with the solemn chants of three priests who beseeched the Divine for my restoration.

In this intertwined dance of realms — where I traversed paradises and ethereal libraries, and they stood vigil in hospital corridors — a testament to faith, strength, and the unwavering bonds that tie us to the tapestry of life unfolded. The echoes of prayers and the commitment of those who stood by me created a narrative of triumph over adversity, laying the foundation for a life redefined.

In the intricate dance between life and death, the hero of my story emerged in the form of a Doctor loyal and devoted to excellence. An excellent neurosurgeon whose unreluctantly determination and groundbreaking medical breakthrough became the catalyst for my miraculous survival. My Doctor personifies strength, confidence, and an unyielding will, especially when it comes to the practice of medicine.

The turning point in my saga came with the emergence of a novel procedure, a medical breakthrough that had never been attempted before. This procedure involved the delicate coiling and stenting of a ruptured brain aneurysm, a technique that held immense potential but was met with skepticism from senior neurologists. My doctor, however, was not one to be deterred by challenges. Fueled by his steadfast belief in the procedure's efficacy and his stubborn belief in his own confidence and his abilities, he embarked on a relentless battle to secure the right to perform this groundbreaking intervention.

The resistance my doctor faced from the medical establishment could have been enough to dissuade a less determined individual. However, armed with a conviction that echoed through every fiber of his being, he fought for the opportunity to pioneer this procedure that held the promise of transforming the landscape of aneurysm treatment. His persistence and tenacity prevailed, and he was granted the green light to embark on this uncharted medical journey.

The pivotal moment arrived when my doctor, armed with innovation and a surgeon's precision, successfully coiled and stented the ruptured aneurysm that had threatened my life. The procedure ensured my survival and paved the way for a life of unparalleled vitality. Physically, mentally, and emotionally, I emerged fully functional, a testament to the transformative power of my doctor's groundbreaking approach.

The impact of this medical breakthrough extended far beyond the confines of my personal narrative. My doctor's success became a beacon of hope for the medical community. Initially met with skepticism, the procedure evolved into a paradigm-shifting advancement in aneurysm treatment. With a 100% success rate in my case, the procedure has since been disseminated, taught, and replicated by my doctor and his peers. The ripple effect of my harrowing experience and my Doctor's courage to challenge convention has propelled the medical field into a new era of life-saving possibilities.

The legacy of this medical breakthrough is etched not only in my renewed lease on life but in the countless lives that have been and will be saved by the hands that dared to be innovative. My Doctor's will and courage to take risks have not only redefined the narrative of my survival but have illuminated a path toward hope and healing for countless others, leaving an indelible mark on the chronicle records of medical history.

As the nurses detected my awakening, the narrative of my life-altering incident unfolded. A commotion of information from medical professionals, family, and friends painted a picture of a journey I had unknowingly embarked upon. It was an overwhelming revelation, a surreal moment where reality collided with the unknown, leaving me to resonate with the gravity of my circumstances.

The shock set in as the details crystallized—the fine thread I treaded between life and death, the severity of the brain aneurysm, and the delicate balance I unknowingly maintained. Yet, panic eluded me. Grounded in humility and a profound realism, I embraced the belief that life happens not "to" us but "for" us. The aneurysm, a forceful pause, redirected the trajectory of my life. It was a necessary intervention to jolt me out of the self-imposed trance, a reminder that, amidst providing for everyone else, I needed to provide for myself. This event catalyzed personal growth, resilience, and a wake-up call echoing far beyond my individual journey— a ripple effect touching all the lives of those who witnessed my miraculous survival.

Words fall short for the gratitude I hold for my parents and their love, faith, and belief in my recovery, my doctor's skill, knowledge and confidence, my sister whose bravery exceeded her own perception, and my brother-in-law who sent me to the right hospital, along with all the family and friends whose prayers were heard so powerfully. Their collective devotion, time, and love stitched the tapestry of my recovery.

My survival was merely the opening act. The real work begins from here. The work of self-reflection and a cleansing deep within the recesses of my core. Gratitude and forgiveness became the cornerstone of my second chance at life. This transformation demanded a thorough self-assessment, a disposal of old belief systems, and the installation of new and improved frameworks for growth. A deep sense of faith, trust, and prayer strengthens my body, mind, and soul.

A new and refreshed relationship formed between my daughters and I and the joy of remarriage came around the corner to complete our family unit. Yet amidst the happiness another life-happening struck the family, my father's passing and the sorrow that followed. He was a pillar of strength that laid the foundation for my journey of becoming who I am today.

In this second lease in life, I discovered a profound calling —a purpose woven into the fabric of my being. My commitment transcends the ordinary, a mission to be a catalyst for changing people's lives. To be a beacon of light illuminating the path for those navigating the often-rough waters of life. A commitment I made to contribute to a collective upliftment—a ripple effect that echoes through communities, fostering positive change on a broader scale around the world. Even after my time on earth has expired.

In conclusion, my journey, marked by an aneurysm and a 21-day nap, has evolved into a transformative odyssey— a testament to the resilience of a human spirit. Practicing gratitude, forgiveness, self-assessment and self-improvement, strengthening your body, mind and soul and fortifying it all with faith, trust and prayer — you have a sure recipe for achieving your greatest heart's desire. Almost like magic.

My everlasting wish and heart desires to change lives and transform hearts so that humanity may ascend into their next greater good to live their best life ever for the rest of their lives.

Jacquellene Lukich is a devoted wife, loving mother, loyal sister, trusted friend, and ambassador of the Most High God. Jacquellene is a seasoned Business Mentor, Breakthrough Expert, NLP Master, Feng Shui Master, Numerologist, Leadership Advisor, Business Strategist, and Relationship Therapist. With over 28+ years of experience, she has helped thousands of businesses and individuals overcome obstacles, break through their limiting beliefs, unlock their true potential, and achieve their goals in record time with long-lasting results and living their best lives. Jacquellene travels the world and speaks multiple languages, giving her a deep appreciation for different cultures and perspectives. Her mission is to empower individuals to live their best life in personal and professional endeavors through proven life-changing tools techniques, and strategies that help her clients achieve success and fulfillment with positive outcomes. Jacquellene's motto is that she changes lives and transforms hearts so people can live their best lives and create a ripple effect across the world.

My Dedication goes to my Family I would not be who I am today for it not for my family. Left to right son-in-law, older daughter, younger daughter, husband, self, Mom, Dad, sister, brother-in-law, niece. I'm a true believer that we DO pick our family. They are the tribe that was assigned to you at birth. You all enter an agreement with one another and walk the journey of life together all the way home. They come with joy, love, dedication, loyalty, devotion, unconditional love and they are the ones to administer the best lessons and guidance in their own special way. And vice-versa. This is what family is all about. Yes, there may be tough days but be rest assured that they will be there through thick and thin. It's just a special LOVE that cannot be bought, you cannot run from it and you can not fool it. It's pure LOVE. I am grateful for each and everyone of them. I am blessed to have such a powerful and loving family in my life.

Living With Integrity
By: Olu Akinruntan

I have been to hell and back, and not all of me made it back. The experience is still all quite fresh, it being only five years or so since it all ended. The scars are still not only fresh, but sore. I am a father of four truly amazing kids, even if quite troublesome at times. The oldest is in her second year of university now, studying Microbiology; my dearest Elizabeth. To me, as must be to all fathers, they are the reason and consolation for all of the sacrifice, struggle and shame borne over the years.

I have been through what was one of the darkest periods that a human being possibly could in life. I know that suffering, struggle, humiliation and shame are relative in the extent to which we experience them. So, having some knowledge of the lives of others means that I have a relatively balanced perspective overall. Between January 2012 and July 2019, I had the most crushing and devastating experience of my life which led to what seemed like my being broken into an untold number of smithereens, and then slowly and painfully being put back together without all the weak and flawed bits.

It began one morning when I got to work where I was responsible for the branding of three subsidiaries of a bank group with a total capital base of about $3,735,703.45 US Dollars. For the life of me, I cannot remember the exact time on that day because it all seems to be in a kind of haze now that I try to recall it. Anyway, at some point, someone came and told me that HR wanted to see me. Of course, that is almost never a good sign, which is even more so in this case, because the bank was going through some upheavals. That was because the group chairman had embezzled about one billion USD and, to get a lesser sentence, she entered a plea bargain with the commission prosecuting frauds.

When I got to HR, the head handed me a sealed envelope and we exchanged a few words, as she was someone that I was kind of close to. I used to help her with her non-work laptops and so on. As I walked away, I opened it and read the letter in it. I don't think anyone ever could adequately capture the feeling that I had at that moment. It was kind of like air was taken away from being able to enter my nostrils. It seemed there was a bright white light that formed behind my eyes and in my head. I felt faint without really having any conscious knowledge of why.

Fear is real, and I was gripped by fear and something close to the worst kind of sensation of being lost or drowning that I have ever felt in my life. The thoughts that were going through my mind included, *"How do I tell my wife? How will the development scare her? How do we survive? What do I do? How do I pay the school fees for my daughter's private school?"*

I followed the instructions in the letter and handed over all items in my possession that belonged to the company, such as the specialized computer system that had been ordered for me from New Jersey, my identity card, keys to the official car and so on. I ensured that the items were signed for by the HR and took my leave. And, after four years and about ten months, that was it.

I went to the small mall across from the office and bought a bottle of Schweppes tonic water and just sat down for a few minutes. I was just trying to recover from the devastating and crippling shock. My mind felt as if it was a highway with vehicles going in every single direction at very high speeds and likely to run into each other at any second, yet never doing. It was exhausting.

Eventually, I got up and headed home. I watched a movie to help calm my nerves. Gradually, I mentally eased into my new reality, letting go of those nerves. I had something to eat, then went to bed. When I woke up, I began to make plans as to how to proceed at that point, to move forward and secure a new means of livelihood, because I had two kids to provide for.

I learnt over the days after that fateful day, how truly blessed I had been all those years being employed because, despite my submitting several applications, I got no other opportunity and my severance pay was fast running out. I walked so far to search for jobs that my shoes had holes in them. When it rained, the water would get through and soak my socks, giving me that horribly uncomfortable squishy feeling as I walked.

Finally, I sold my official car which I had been able to buy off the company at a highly discounted rate, according to company policy. I used some of the proceeds to rent an office, hoping that would be better since I wasn't having any luck with securing another employment. Then, I learnt my second lesson, which was how running a business isn't easy by any means, and is an entirely different ball game from being an employee.

Things only got worse as time went on. It always felt like I was in a struggle to the death with poverty. Constantly at the forefront of my mind was the fear of becoming destitute. Eventually, I could no longer continue to pay rent and had to move out. I also had to move out of the apartment that we were living in and into another part of the state that was cheaper. I also felt that, being an area where a lot of real estate construction was ongoing, I'd have better prospects of securing graphic and web design, branding, and computer training opportunities.

Eventually, we ended up in a one-room apartment in 2014, about two years after I lost my job, which shows how quickly the life of a human being can become undone in Nigeria because we have no social welfare structure. I was completely on my own and with no help to get back on my feet. However, I certainly wasn't going to go and just sit down somewhere and wallow in self-pity. I had two kids to provide for, after all.

Sadly however, slowly but surely, our standard of living fell. It got to the point where I owed so many supermarkets and shops that I could only go out when it was dark to avoid being seen by them. For a man such as myself whose dignity mattered, my reality became almost a pure hell. I constantly had to struggle mentally and emotionally with the shame that I felt being in the situation.

No one can truly know our story because the experience of an event by a human being is more than just physical. It is also emotional and psychological. No one can fully understand what we experience emotionally and psychologically as we go through situations. It took the grace of God for me not to just break down under the weight of it all. I had basically become a beggar.

It was the most humiliating experience of my life, and sometimes, just sitting down somewhere all on my own, I wondered how I got into that situation. I intend to never ever do so again now that I'm more knowledgeable with all that I went through back then. I cannot say it's impossible, but Lord knows I am doing whatever else I have to rather than be in such a vulnerable position again.

At one point, two young men approached me and asked me to design a California driver's license for them. They lived in my neighborhood, with one being well-known as a scammer and referred to commonly as a Yahoo Boy. The other, too, was a scammer, but not as "successful" as the former. They came to me because they knew I was very good with computers generally. They offered me enough to keep my kids and I taken care of for at least a month.

The temptation was so powerful because during those

terrible days I was broke as usual and could do with just about any amount of money at all. I mean, I would go to the mosque as early as four in the morning to see if I could catch a Muslim person that I knew or that looked approachable coming out of the mosque after their prayers to ask for money. I'd ask for as little as fifty naira, which was about twenty-five cents around 2014 or so.

So, I really needed the money, especially with two kids that I had to feed and provide for. During those days, I owed school fees all the time because I had no regular source of income. I only had a bit left over now and then when I was blessed enough to have gotten a graphic or web design commission. And, out of the fee, I had to pay off some debts, and buy gasoline to power my generator for electricity so that I could do the work.

I would always agonize over how much to spend on gasoline and Internet subscription so that there would be enough for me to complete the job. Most of the time, I'd pay off some debts in the morning and be right back in the evening to buy on credit again. It was a horrible way to live, and I wouldn't wish it on anyone. Finally, I told them both that I couldn't do it.

A second motivation for telling them "No" was the stories of people who had worked with scammers to forge documents who ended up being arrested and sent to prison when the scammers were caught and told on those people. I wasn't so afraid of or affected by hunger that I'd risk losing my freedom. I also recalled once seeing a young man in handcuffs led by some police men, into an Internet cafe that I had been in years ago.

What would happen to my kids if I was arrested? I mean, it's not as if I was providing the very best quality of life while I was not arrested, but my reasoning was that it certainly would be worse for them if I was. So I made the choice not to take the risk. Years later, I saw one of the two. He didn't seem to have made much progress compared to way back then, but I had moved out of the one-room apartment.

I recall an elderly man and woman also offered to help me out with some voodoo, too, stating that someone who should be living a much better life such as I looked shouldn't be in the condition that I was. To each, I said I'd think about it and never brought up the matter again; whenever I ran into them, they didn't either. I am glad I didn't take that route either, because if I had, they'd have been in a position to say now that they were the ones who helped me using voodoo and I'd have denied God the glory that is rightly His.

I am not home-free, as I still do get broke sometimes. I now have four kids, after all. However, I am definitely not at the abject level that I used to be. That is because now, after years and years of application, sacrifice, living frugally and spending money only on those things that my kids and I needed to stay alive, I began to find opportunities that lasted long enough for us to rise out of poverty each time. One of those opportunities is my being a part of this anthology.

Each time that I secured opportunities, such as my first one with a wonderful lady in El Paso, Texas, I'd scale up my investment in gasoline and Internet subscription. That meant I could stay online and search for opportunities much longer. Then, I had my very first major break in May of 2017 when I was commissioned to design my very first website. I rented a single-bedroom flat which came with a sitting room, bathroom and toilet and kitchen.

For the first time since 2013, I experienced running water again, and will never forget my kids just showering and showering. I used to have to go about two houses away to fetch water from a well. Now, to wash dishes and so on, all the kids had to do was turn on the tap in the kitchen at the sink. I recall once having to use my laptop as collateral to buy some drugs for my son, MacArthur, to be treated for malaria by a nurse at home. I couldn't afford to take him to the hospital since hospitals demand a deposit before even checking vital signs.

Eventually, the nurse ran away when the boy was getting worse and wasn't responding to treatment. I then offered my WiFi modem to the owner of a small clinic who declined saying, "Isn't that what you use for work? If I collect it from you, how would you make money to come and pay me?" I was kind of in shock at hearing another human being say that, because, during those years, I hadn't experienced much kindness at all. She treated him, and almost instantly we could see the change in him. I was able to pay her the next week.

During those days, every single day was a fight to hold on to my dignity and integrity. It seemed every minute was determined to humiliate me and break me down. Once, my landlady, during a particularly tough period, came and sat on a wooden stool in front of my door with my kids inside the one-room apartment and refused to let me come out. Two of my co-tenants begged her with no result.

Miraculously, a man who would always ask me for a quote, yet never gave me a job over the course of several years, called and asked me how much it'd cost to do a 3D modelling of an escarpment over a canal. Needless to say, he agreed to the fee and paid me the following Monday. The fee was at least three times my annual rent. I sent the balance of my rent to the landlady, and added something for her to get chicken for Christmas.

What I learnt in the course of those years in a very real way was how choosing to live with integrity, even though we may suffer more and for longer periods due to passing on opportunities to keep our integrity intact, two things are likely to happen. Number one, we'd come in contact with those who see and value our integrity. Number two, there is a feeling that radiates through the whole of our being that cannot be overlooked, which I think has to do with our psyche being guilt-free because we constantly carry with us the knowledge that we didn't cut corners by defrauding or harming others.

It is why I think some people who end up achieving success and wealth while compromising their integrity seem to have self-destructive tendencies, and engage in activities that indicate low self-esteem, narcissism, and other psycho-emotional fissures in their personality. If you need a friend to walk with you through some challenges, or to share actionable and proven strategies that will help you prepare against, and maybe even prevent some of the unforeseen events that life throws at us sometimes, I'd be honored to be of as much help as I can be.

Transforming Visions into Reality | Creative Designer & Web Guru | Social Media Maverick | Wordsmith | Tech Whiz | Your Virtual Right Hand

With nearly 28 years of experience in graphic and web design, brand communications, social media management, writing, IT support, and since 2019, virtual assistance, I am recognized for my commitment to delivering surpassing value in sustainable ways.

Throughout my career, I have crafted visually compelling designs, executed strategic brand communication campaigns, and driven engagement through effective social media management. My passion for writing has enabled me to articulate captivating narratives, while my IT support expertise ensures seamless operations.

Known for my integrity and dedication to ethical principles, I am committed to making a positive impact through my diverse skill set. Let's connect and explore how I can contribute to your success.

LinkedIn Profile: https://www.linkedin.com/in/seyiakinruntan/

Email Address: seyifulfilled@gmail.com

WhatsApp: +234 905 743 7659

Dedication

I dedicate my chapter to God Almighty above all. My Christian background is the foundation of values and principles that make me a decent human being with uncompromising integrity and compassion. I thank my parents, Fadesola and Elizabeth and my kids, Elizabeth, MacArthur, Maximus and MacArdell who have made it all more than worth it in a way that's pure magic. There is a motivation in my relationship with them that I cannot explain.

I thank all those who have been of help to me on my journey such as Dr. Constance Leyland, Stanley Greene, Kimberly Woodruff, Bobbi Malanowski, Omar M, Wale Kadri, Wole Ladipo and Sandra Dee Richardson, whom I seem to run into as if they were asked to be at those points where I'd really need some relief seeming to confirm to me that I must be doing something right. Thank you all.

Serendipitous Souls: A Military Spouse Journey!

By: Laurie Manibusan

I love the movie *"Serendipity"*. I especially love the movie quote; *"If we're to meet again, then we'll meet again. It's just not the right time now."* That movie and quote resonates with me because of my life coming full circle in reuniting with my husband Joe, a dedicated Veteran, who has served 37 years with the Army, and who I consider my best friend and soulmate.

Joe and I went to high school together in Guam. I left him during my 10th grade year in 1984 bound for California to pursue my education. I never got a chance to tell him I was leaving for California the day he almost landed a kiss on me while taking me down from the bleachers due to the rain. I was shocked by his attempt and ran away. I thought to myself, *"How could he try to kiss me after all these years as friends?" Why now?*

While being away from Guam, I often thought about that moment, and felt I should have told him how I truly felt for him too, but my mom and stepfather were very strict about dating during high school and my only reaction was to run. Besides, I was leaving, so what's the point in telling him?

Fast forward 2 years later in 1987, after graduating from high school in California, I returned to my Island of Guam at the request of my mother, Dorothy. I never imagined meeting up with Joe again, considering he left for boot camp after he graduated in 1986. Unbeknownst to me, he had returned from bootcamp in the Summer of 1987, and we accidentally bumped into each other at Gibson's Dept Store. He asked me to lunch, reminded me of the *"almost kiss"* moment and the rest was history. Joe and I have been together for 37 years. We have three beautiful children, Nico Jude, J'Nisha Jolani, and Ian Joseph. We also have three precious grandchildren, *Emmett, Eivor, and Eagan*, from our son Nico and Daughter-in-law Taryn; and a fur-baby grand pug named *Pickles* that belongs to J'Nisha and Joshua.

Conceiving our first-born son at the age of twenty-one was a trying time because of the surgery I endured to remove his twin from my Fallopian tube, yet I managed to carry him full term. Nico was known as our miracle baby. In 2011, our son decided to follow in his dad's footsteps and joined the Army. He had been serving for 13 years and managed to get his degree in the process. He married his childhood friend, and they blessed us with our grandchildren.

Our daughter J'Nisha has always excelled in her studies and is a Physician Associate and married her true love Joshua, who is a successful Chemical Engineer. Jay and Josh knew that they had to focus on finishing their college and if they were meant to be they could handle a long-distance relationship that resulted in lasting 8 years and a happy ending being married in the eyes of our lord savior on May 13, 2023. The day of our daughter's wedding was the best Mother's Day gift for me considering 2021 Mother's Day was a heartbreaking time with my sisters Nancy and Del and nieces Francesca and Dottie when we were dressing my mother Dorothy for her funeral services. That will be the saddest day engrained in our hearts.

Our youngest son Ian wants to pursue a career in being a Lineman and is dating a beautiful, intelligent athlete named Callie, who he considers his best friend in high school. Ian has always had a big heart and loves carving. He is always willing to help others too. Though I am fearful of his chosen career path, I just got to support his decision and pray for his safety always.

We are extremely proud of our children. We love them equally and look forward to their continued successes and aspirations. Parents always pray that their kids will grow up to be responsible citizens, find their true calling, and love of their lives.

However, my life has not always been a fairy tale. Being a spouse of a Veteran for 37 years has taught me a lot about sacrifices, dedication, commitment, resilience, and heartache. I often ask myself how I survived all the bumps in the road and the answer *"The grace of our Lord Savior"* and my own upbringing from the strongest women I know, my **MOM!**

Mom was always an industrious worker and sacrificed a lot for her 12 children. She lived through the Japanese Occupation, worked the farm, took care of her own two siblings Danny and Annie, experienced a tragic fall that broke her back and left her paralyzed, yet she fought to recover, besides, she had kids to care for. Being the youngest in my family, I learned a lot about life and what to do and not do from my siblings. They always protected me, and I love them with all my heart. Growing up we bounced back and forth to the mainland and to Guam. I got the best of both worlds. Understanding the Island living and culture versus the mainland way of life made me appreciate our Chamorro Culture even more. Well, it was my time to be the wife, mother, diligent worker that our mom raised me to become.

When the Iraq war broke out in 2003, we were living on Guam. I knew Joe would eventually have to deploy to defend our country and fight for our freedom. Guam is especially important to the military because of its geographic position in the Pacific and the role it plays in national defense supporting both air, land, and sea for the Western Pacific region.

In 2005, Joe was off to rebuild as an Engineer with the 411th Charlie Company USAR. He deployed for 18 months to Iraq when Ian was only a few months old. When Joe returned, Ian was turning 2 years old, J'Nisha was eight and Nico was thirteen. Though he lost 18 months of his kids' lives, I made sure the kids did not lose hope and faith that their dad would be home soon. It was also incredibly challenging that year because his mother had breast cancer and was flown from the Island to Los Angeles for Chemo and radiation treatment. Life needed to go on without Joe being home and I had to stabilize the Homefront as much as possible. We kept busy and active, especially with the Family Readiness Group (FRG). The kids and I looked forward to the day he would come back from Iraq for his R&R leave, which was genuinely nice to have him home for one Christmas.

Joe always knew the month of December has always been hard for me because I was reliving the frightful moment of December 12,1985 when my brother Manuel, a dedicated Guam Police Officer, and a Military Police (MP) for the Army, who was tragically taken from us. On December 21, 1985, my brother's burial was on my not so Sweet 16 birthday. After his death, our family was never the whole. Manuel had a wife and a one-year daughter at the time of his death. I never wanted to celebrate my birthdays since his death and always wanted December to come and go quickly, as to not feel the pain of losing him all over again. Not only did we have New Years to follow without him, but once again feeling the pain the day after, since it was Manny's birthday on January 2nd, with mom's birthday being January 12th. As the years passed, we also mourn the death of three other brothers Johnny, Alfred, and Alex, who passed away from illnesses and our matriarch, Dorothy and father Johnny.

I began actively pursuing my role as an FRG Leader with the 411ᵗʰ, moved on to be a certified Senior Volunteer Instructor for the 9ᵗʰ RSC Command USARC with the help of our 9ᵗʰ RSC Family Program Director, Col. Kim Goffar, who inspired me every step of the way. Kim was not only a brave soldier who served her country, but a cancer survivor. She was my mentor, friend, a sister in Christ and became a part of my own family. I gave 9 years in leading such a dynamic group of families and worked with many fine, strong women (*Laurie, Ana, Tina, Christina, Francis, Jeannette, Josette, Daniele, and a male spouse Kelly*) who held main roles in the FRG Group. It was a team effort to take care of our soldiers and families of Charlie Company. We were known as "Charlies Angels" from the 9ᵗʰ RSC. We also had an exceptionally good young Commander at the time, Col. Jason Guerrero. Growing up, Jason, would share with us that he was a product of the FRG, and he had a vision to carry on the same commitment of utilizing the FRG to help with the stresses of deployments, reunions, transitions, and just to promote resilience within our families and soldiers alike, because of his parents.

In 2002, Jason's wife, Laurie Guerrero who was our Vice President of the FRG Group, along with me flew to the Pentagon to bring home the DoD Reserve Family Readiness Award on behalf of the Charlie Company 411ᵗʰ Engineer Battalion Guam. On Feb. 15, 2002, Craig W. Duehring, Principal Deputy Assistant Secretary of Defense for Reserve Affairs, presented the award. This was a prestigious award, and it was the first competition that DOD had announced. We were overly excited that we won as all our hard work in support of our soldiers and families paid off through humble recognition. Considering this was after 9-11, receiving this award on behalf of our FRG Group for their sacrifice and dedication was a bittersweet moment for us. It was very memorable and solemn and impacted me in many ways.

I could not focus on the award at that time, as thoughts of the lives that were tragically taken, people in mourning, a time to heal, and a city to rebuild were crashing hard over me. It was that moment that reminded me why I dedicated my life to helping others as a public servant both in the civilian world and military world.

This was another busy chapter of my life of supporting military families and doing everything I could in my role as a Family Readiness Group Leader along with our FRG main members to conduct our mission of family support for 9 years. We provided training for military families and soldiers on diverse topics like Suicide Prevention, Transitions, Deployments, Finance, AR-608 roles and rules, planning many fundraising events to hosts holiday meals, gifts for Soldiers children, and trying to promote resiliency in any way possible to our military families. We partook with all other military branches in promoting the Purple Ribbon Campaign on the Island until all our deployed soldiers came home safely.

Deployments are extremely difficult for families and soldiers to deal with. For some spouses, deployments tore them apart and led to divorce, some mourned the loss of their loved one, and for others it strengthened their bond in marriage. Thankfully, the Army provided the Strong Bond Retreat for couples and for single soldiers upon returning home from deployments and even prior to deployments. Those types of training are critical and useful especially for young couples and newlyweds. It also gave a sense of anew to those who have been married longer with their spouse.

However, the fear of a soldier not returning home due to a casualty can leave a family crushed, angered, broken, unanchored, and their whole life upside down. The broken pieces of their heart, ripped from their body, is an unbearable pain to fathom. Even though our brave military personnel would say, *"We know and understand the risk when we raised our right hand and took an oath to protect and fight for our freedom..."*, It's still hard on military families to succumb to such fear, especially during deployments. I felt for my husband who had to be a Casualty Assistance Officer for a fallen soldier. It was even harder to bear because the soldier who was killed in Iraq was the son of my daughter's elementary teacher and that hit too close to home for our own daughter and for us.

The Army has taken us to 11 duty stations. We started out in our home of record, Guam, then Fort Jackson, South Carolina, Fort Irwin, and Fort Hunter Liggett both in California, Lima Ohio, Joint Base Lewis McChord, Washington State, Fort Bliss, El Paso Texas, Fort Leonard Wood, Missouri, and Fort Belvoir, Virginia. Each duty station we had to relocate has been an experience that we will not forget. We met many great friends and families that made the Army life and transitioning into a new place a vast experience and became our extended family.

Relocating every year to two years in general can be daunting and exhausting, but you cannot let that break your spirit or bring on undue stress on your mental health. It makes you fatigued and can put stress on your body of unpacking and packing all over again. There are times you do not want to even unpack everything because you know you are going to move within a short amount of time, so you unpack the necessities. I came to the realization that if you do not need it, get rid of it. Someone else might need it and you do not need to be dragging it along every duty station or keeping it in storage or boxed up. Trust me, I learned the hard way! However, I am on a journey to do so as we near retirement for Joe.

I often think if we did not move to South Carolina, our

oldest son, Nico, would not have joined the Army himself and wouldn't have rekindled his friendship online with his wife Taryn. Our middle child, J'Nisha, would not have met Joshua, her soulmate and now husband, in California. Our youngest son, Ian, would not have met his best friend and love of his life, Callie in Missouri. Therefore, I say "Serendipity" has occurred for not only myself, but my children.

I am thankful for surviving all the PCS moves that we endured because of the Army. It has brought not only life experiences and adventures to our children, but they are able to see the world through many lenses. They are also resilient when it comes to life changes. The many elementary, middle schools, high schools they had to attend in such a brief period and one of them experienced homeschool on top of that for a year, just made them resilient. They were very sad when they would have to pick up and leave their friends and go to another state and rebuild new friendships, but they did it and survived the mix of emotions and uncertainties not by choice but because they had to support their father's duty as an American Soldier.

Today, the kids are very appreciative as they are older and wiser to understand the service and sacrifice that their father has done for them and what the Army has provided for them. Life is full of surprises, especially when you are a military spouse. However, you must remain positive when the negative is pounding at your doorstep. You must protect your mental, physical, spiritual health and well-being. We must remind ourselves we can do it and we can do it together! You are not alone as other military spouses are trying to survive the best way they can. You need to find that support system. I hear you; I see you and I believe in you! I am here for you!

I always loved this quote, *"Behind every strong soldier, there is an even stronger woman who stands behind him, supports him, and loves him with all her heart."*

However, there are single soldiers and members of our LGTBQ community who proudly serve as well. Therefore, I even love this quote even more, *"Behind every strong military member, there is a support system that believes in them, prays for them, cooks for them, and loves them unconditionally with all their hearts."*

I lost a loved-one in every duty station, and if you felt the same loss, keep their memories alive as you continue in service and sacrifice for your soldier, your family, community, and country. Stay resilient! Find your passion, follow your dreams, share it with the world, be there for someone who is in need, be that mentor, inspire with love, care, and trust. You have a story to be told and light to shine for when others feel it is dim. You never know what families are going through, so remember to be kind! Love one Another! We have enough hate, racism, crime, and chaos in this world. Why add to that life when you can instill peace, joy, happiness and grow as a village in caring for each other's children and be there for others when you can.

In closing, I like to share my personal affirmations in surviving as a military spouse:

1. You are never alone; others are going through the exact same thing.
2. Ask for help, seek help, and embrace help.
3. Find your happy place and indulge in your self-care.
4. If your plate is full, then share the responsibility with others who will help you finish what is on your plate.
5. There is always a higher being, give it all to him in prayer.

6. Find your War-room and let it be a place of serenity.
7. If you opened your eyes today, be thankful as someone else did not have that opportunity to be here on earth again.
8. You are the backbone of the family, how you feel they will feel, therefore, keep positive and motivate them to do well with life changes.
9. Changes in life are inevitable, it is how you sail your ship and how you anchor it too, besides you are the captain of your own Ship, called *"Life!"*.
10. Most especially, Protect your Mental Health, Physical Health, and Spiritual Health.

As you journey forward, may you encounter unexpected blessings coordinated with divine timing. Wishing your life is finest, I stand resilient as a military spouse, my spirit unbroken beside my soldier. He is ready to sacrifice for family, country, and liberty. Let the Lord's grace accompany you, blessings to your kin, praying for guardianship over our service members, solace for the bereaved, and safety for those facing peril. May peace prevail.

Laurie Manibusan is a long-time educator and public servant. Most importantly she is a proud military spouse to a Veteran serving 37 years in the Army and a proud mother of 3 children and 3 grandchildren. Her passion for serving military families and supporting soldiers stemmed from leading a group of strong spouses as a former Family Readiness Group Leader, a Senior Volunteer Resource Instructor, FPAC Member, and Senior Spouse Advisor. Laurie is the proud spouse of Sergeant Major Joseph Manibusan.

She is a graduate of the University of Guam, a former Chief of Staff, and USO Board Member on Guam. Laurie is an instructor with Laurus College under the Professional Business Systems. Her passion for teaching and helping others achieve their success and aspirations is her top priority.

To my hero SGM Joseph Manibusan and beloved family; Nico Jude & Taryn (*Emmett, Eivor & Eagan*), J'Nisha Jolani & Joshua (*Pickles*), and Ian Joseph & Callie, as well as to my Mother Dorothy, and the Charlie's Angels (411th USAR FRG Group),

Your unwavering love and support are what binds my story in so many ways. May the words in this chapter serve as a testament of how strong you can be to overcome any obstacles that life throws at you. The good Lord blessed me with many individuals that have inspired me along my life's journey. I vow to do the same for others. Thank you for your unselfish sacrifices you also have endured to support your father's career. Dad and I are so proud of you kids and love you with all our hearts and soul. Always stay humble and kind. Keep God in your life always. Love Always, Mom!

Somewhere in Between

By: Danielle Castañeda Manaois

On the car ride to the Emergency Room (ER), I remember saying to myself, "I think he is going to die" and feeling overwhelmed with uneasiness and fear. I repeated to myself, "God please bless us." I recalled every few minutes reaching for my husband's hand attempting to hide my worst fear - him dying. As cars passed by, I glanced at him every few moments and out of concern, told him to repeatedly squeeze my hand. In response, his squeeze was weak and I did my best to hold back tears. Thinking back to that day I had no idea that this day would shake our world and force me to thrive where I feel the most comfortable, the grey zone.

In a society that often sees things in black and white, I invite you to shift your perspective and embrace the grey zone – a place where ambiguity is not an adversary but an ally. In this insightful narrative, we embark on a journey beyond the rigidity of societal norms, challenging the biases that bind us and seeking a deeper understanding of our multifaceted reality. As we explore the grey zone in life and business, we uncover the profound power of empathy, not only as a moral compass, but as a strategic force capable of transforming organizations from the inside out. My story is a testament to thriving in uncertainty, leading with the heart, and finding strength somewhere in between.

My words are not just a reflection but a call to action for leaders and individuals to embrace the complexities of life and discover the unexpected opportunities that lie within. When I think of thriving in life's grey zone, I think of it as a choice. To thrive is to choose that despite the uncertainty of life and the hardships that come your way, that we have a choice to survive or thrive. My choice is to thrive. To embrace and live in gratefulness, mindfulness, and to lead and communicate with empathy.

To live beyond boundaries is to embrace a different way of thinking. The grey zone juxtaposes the overwhelming comfort of dichotomies. Yes or no. Black or white. Right or wrong. This or that. The grey embraces the yes, the no, and some version in between. The grey is a combination of two sides, another version of what is to be expected and a departure from dichotomy.

At Castaneda and Manaois Consulting (CMC), we embrace the grey zone and center around people first. We strongly believe that an organization's strongest asset is people. We are passionate about empowering businesses to consider leading and communicating with empathy. We believe that when people are heart-centered it can transform organizations.

While the heart may be routinely foreign to business operations, think of the heart and empathy as a source of strength, to give life to your core values and what your business stands for. If we think of empathy as an opportunity to seek deeper understanding, empathy can be a bridge to more.

It is also a foreign concept to consider a time of strife and turmoil as a blessing. Times of uncertainty are often labeled as tumultuous and have a negative connotation. But the uneasiness of uncertainty can be formative, a time of reinvention, reflection, and an opportunity to give meaning to life and motivation to continue.

This idea and concept to accept one's journey, to ride life's waves of uncertainty and embrace the choice to see the silver lining and see uncertainties and unknowns as a blessing are what I believe it means to thrive in the grey zone. Everyday we have a choice to redefine and reframe our worlds, to choose to thrive.

So, what is the importance of this in business or in the grand scheme of life? My answer would be that there is not always a definitive answer. The lesson or value of something is not always clear.

On January 15, 2024, my husband tested positive for COVID-19. At the time, I was unaware that this would cause ripples that would shape our family's life moving forward. On January 18, 2024, after texting his boss, he turned over to ask me to drop our three children, heard a click in his head then the world started spinning. After I dropped the kids, I knew something was wrong. This prompted me to call the advice nurse. After reporting that he had a high blood pressure, low temperature, and low pulse, the nurse would recommend going to the ER.

As we were preparing to leave for the hospital, my husband was dizzy, nauseated, and had a huge headache. As he was getting up from our bed, he fell. So, I draped my 5'10, 280 pound husband over my 4'11 frame and headed to the ER.

That day we would spend seven or more hours in the ER. I remember it being packed and barely where to sit. In a sea of sick patients my husband would stand out, immobilized in the wheelchair barely responding to my repeated ask if he was ok. When they called his name to triage him, we would tell the staff what we told the nurse over the phone and they would tell us it was probably symptoms from COVID. We were sent back to a sea of sick people to sit for the duration of the seven hour day.

After more than five hours we would be taken into an ER room where they would barely provide care. I cannot even remember the Physician's Assistant coming back to explain what happened or what to do. Even after we pleaded for more answers, my husband would leave that ER, still nauseated, dizzy, unstable, and blood pressure high. The image of my husband in the wheelchair not moving or talking still makes me shudder.

By January 21st, he remained in the same state and I was increasingly concerned his disposition was not getting better. Out of fear of receiving the same treatment I strapped my husband almost a foot taller than me and almost twice my weight and we headed out. This time we would go to the Urgent Care. Again we would sit almost an hour waiting for him to get care. When we were seen they would find my husband still unable to walk, still dizzy, huge headache, pulse low, and blood pressure high. After trying to stabilize his blood pressure, the doctor would apologize and send us to the ER for a hypertensive emergency.

When we arrived in the early evening of January 21st, the hospital was busier than January 18th although this time my husband was immediately taken to do an EKG. This time they triaged quickly and took back to a room in the ER. Again, we would sit. We would explain the same thing, get the same explanations, run the same tests, and receive no clarity what was going on with my husband

In desperation for answers, I would advocate for my husband that something was not right. I advocated that the intervention and steps taken on January 18th did not help. Again we would tell them of his excruciating headache and finally on January 22nd, he finally got a CT.

I remember this doctor coming into our room and explaining that the CT revealed a blood clot. Later that morning, we found out that he suffered a stroke. As the doctor explained that it likely happened a week prior, everything started flooding together. When the doctor asked where we were after the stroke - we explained we were in that same ER. I was in complete shock.

At this point, I felt like I was having an out of body experience. How could my 43 year old husband suffer a stroke? Not only that, we were told that there wasn't anything besides dispensing medicine, intensive rehabilitation, and monitoring my husband would be all that could be done. We learned that the time had passed for intervention of the stroke with any medication or surgery because the damage was done. It was too late. To make matters worse, we would learn that he didn't just have one stroke, but two.

The point of this sad story and the weight of what is our family's reality: in the case of my husband and that fateful January 18th - if the medical team acted and communicated with empathy that day, would my husband's outcome be different? Was there something keeping the staff from treating my husband with respect?

While I believe that we have every right to ask for answers, to grieve the life or quality of life he could have had if intervention had taken place on January 18th, I choose to see the silver lining. Despite the overwhelming sadness we feel at times, we chose to continue praying for his recovery and recognizing the blessing that my husband is still with us. To choose to thrive is to accept that sadness can exist with gratefulness. There is no right or wrong to some questions in life and in business, it is complex at times, it is embracing and moving with the changes, and riding the ebb and flow of life.

Fast forward to January 28, 2024, after visiting my husband, my daughter and I came home. Like most four-year-olds, she had overcome her tears from leaving her dad at the hospital temporarily and found her bubbly as ever. While eating, I could see my daughter in peripheral saw and heard her laughing and then a huge thump.

My daughter jumped, missed my sibling's hand, and landed on the back of her head. Unlike so many accidents before, there was no cry. As I quickly glanced down I noticed her face turn bright red. In desperation, I remember begging her, "Elize, move your head babe!" My mom and my sibling frantically attempted to keep her awake calling out her name, "Elize! Elize! Wake up." The image of her, once bubbly little frame and so full of just hung for minutes, her eyes rolling back in my siblings arms, lifeless. Those minutes felt like a lifetime. As my mom and sibling attempted to keep her awake, and when she was not responding I dialed 911. Once again, I was thinking, "God, please bless us."

When the first responders arrived, they handled it similarly to the treatment my husband received in the ER on January 18th. In comparison, the Emergency Medical Technicians (EMT) would respond differently.

In comparison to my husband's first visit to the ER my daughter were in and out in less than four hours. The staff would spend that time monitoring, medicating, and running a computed tomography (CT) scan. The doctors listened and treated us with respect and validated my daughter's and my fear. They would ease my fears by informing me of how I should proceed in the next week and what we should look out for. All in all, she would leave with a hematoma and concussion. I would leave comforted in the information and the care we received.

My experience with my daughter on January 28th in comparison to my experience with my husband on January 18th and why they were treated so differently is not clear. My thought is, on January 28th, while doing what was medically necessary, they communicated with empathy. I do not feel that I need to ask the staff on January 28th, if they would act differently if it were their child. I am glad there is no need to.

If we were to approach work with both our expertise and also treat others with the utmost love and care – it could transform our workplaces, our relationships in and outside of work, our workplaces, our communities, and the world.

You have 24 hours in the day, are you making the best

of it? Are you making a positive impact? Do you lead with empathy? If the staff acted differently on January 18th, my husband's outcome and quality of life may be different.

If you are a business owner, ask yourself if you approach your life and workplace with that mindset to start with your heart and thrive in the grey zone. If so, the results of shedding our conscious and unconscious bias coupled with empathy can be transformative. Transforming organizations when you start with your heart and lead with empathy can steer organizations to think about more than just the bottom line but the value of putting people first.

It is ok to be dedicated to putting pieces back together and feel like everything is falling apart. Despite the challenges or degrees of difficulty that you face in life and in business, position yourself to receive light.

To thrive in the grey is to recognize that business challenges often do not have a single solution or outcome. Rather, there may be multiple solutions and varying degrees of outcomes just like life. I encourage you to embrace the spectrum of possibilities and challenge you to the thought that emotions and responses can be varied. It is not about right or wrong, but navigating and embracing the in-between. Businesses must be willing to operate with transparency. Businesses must find comfort, opportunity in the strategic advantages in the space where answers are nuanced, where solutions and outcomes are somewhere in between.

Danielle Manaois is co-owner and Chief Executive Officer (CEO) of Castañeda & Manaois Consulting (CMC). CMC specializes in simplifying the intricate maze of workplace challenges and prides themselves on casting clarity in the complexity of the workplace. As experts in Human Resources, we provide straightforward and effective solutions that steer organizations toward success.

CMC believes that empowering leaders to start with their hearts and lead with empathy is essential to transform organizations and work cultures to increase their overall organizational health and can have a powerful impact on productivity, efficiency, etc.

Danielle Castañeda Manaois' mission is to leave a legacy for her children that her hard work will empower them to seek their passion in an impactful and intentional way. This is her way of leaving the world a better place than she found it, through her children and generations to come. Further it is her hope that they will continue a legacy of starting with their hearts and leading with empathy.

Danielle dedicates this chapter to her loving husband that he may find peace in their new normal. She thanks him for his dedication to their faith, perseverance, and resilience to continue to progress everyday and to find the blessings somewhere in between.

The New Beginning

By: Kristin Lynne Nori

The air smelled stale, and the room was overheated as I rushed into the staff meeting from afternoon bus duty. My cheeks were bright red from the cold winter air being met with the room's heat. As I walked in, the principal told the staff he was disappointed with the fidelity of interventions, especially on the behavioral side. It immediately struck a nerve with me because I was the coordinator for this.

Yet despite being in charge of coordinating and providing many of these interventions, I had spent the entire day subbing in sixth grade for a teacher who was out sick, which was not my choice. Walking into that staff meeting and hearing the public criticism about interventions not being done hit me like a ton of bricks. I always look to be an overachiever at my job. In this situation, I felt publicly called out for not performing. This was December 2, 2021, and COVID-19 had taken its toll on all educators that year.

I was angry, irate. I could feel my blood pressure rising, and my heart began to race. My colleague, who knows me well, put her hand on top of mine to try to calm me, but all this did was to bring all of my emotions bubbling to the surface, and I began crying in front of the entire staff. I excused myself quickly, but I was upset. As a support staff member during a teacher shortage, I subbed for absent teachers more than I could do my job.

Despite that, my principal continued business as usual, as though my feelings were invalid. Besides filling out my primary job requirements, I was asked to substitute on this day. This made my workday longer and more stressful. I had always been a team player and jumped to offer help, so I felt punched in the gut as though my efforts to help the team were not appreciated.

219

When I left the building that evening, it was already dark, and I had also arrived in the dark that morning. I had served morning duty, covered a class for someone else all day (canceling my interventions), and then served afternoon bus duty before attending our staff meeting. I was overworked, exhausted, and suffering from severe anxiety and depression.

I looked over at the school as I got into my car, and the tears instantly began to pour out again. I didn't know if I could return to work after 22 years of working in public education. Ironically, this was the night before what was to be the start of my 23rd year. Instead of celebrating, I went home and told my partner that I could not go to work the next day and that I wasn't sure when I would return because of my mental health and wellness suffering. I am blessed that he was very supportive of my decision.

As someone who has been a teacher for over twenty-five years, I watched the job evolve and change. At first, my primary responsibility was to teach the students. Still, as time passed, I took on additional roles and responsibilities. I had to be a jack of all trades, taking on the roles of mentor, counselor, tutor, researcher, assessor, leader, cheerleader, interventionist, and curriculum specialist, to name just a few. Each role required a unique skill set, and I had to adapt to each one accordingly. As a mentor, I had to be a role model for my students, guiding them through academic and personal challenges. In contrast, as a tutor, I had to provide individualized instruction to help students.

As a special educator, my responsibilities were even more complex. Besides the roles above, I had to be an expert in various disabilities and the best practices for helping all students grow, and understanding such a vast amount required a deep understanding of the unique challenges that students with different disabilities face and the tools and techniques needed to support them. I also had to be an expert in special education law to ensure my students and their paperwork complied with federal regulations.

As the job morphed over time, the lines between these roles and responsibilities became increasingly blurry, and it became more challenging to navigate the shades of grey that emerged. Nevertheless, I remained committed to providing the best possible education to my students and helping them succeed in every way possible.

After spending many years feeling like I was spinning my wheels and not making a significant enough impact, I decided to step away from public education. This decision was among the hardest I have ever made, as I had never imagined myself doing anything other than working in the general education sector. As I looked for jobs I was qualified for, I realized I did not have to leave my work in education after all. Instead of working on the inside, I devoted the rest of my life to helping improve the broken United States educational system- from the outside.

I started to look at the grey area for answers to the pain points in our educational system. Using outside-of-the-box thinking allowed me to create ideas for improving our educational system. We commonly classify things in absolute terms, often in black and white, suitable and wrong, left and right, yes and no. However, the in-between, or the grey area, always falls in the middle of these absolutes. Things are not strictly one way or the other in the grey zone, but a combination. When we think outside the box, it often provides a unique perspective or solution that is not readily apparent when only considering the extremes.

It was a stroke of fate when I connected with Christine Lynn Jones, whose guidance helped me realize the validity and feasibility of my ideas and dreams. We met on LinkedIn when our mutual friends urged us to read each other's posts and articles. We resonated with every idea and notion as we delved into each other's thoughts. It was only natural that we decided to set up a video chat, and from the moment we started talking, we clicked like two halves of a whole. We finished each other's sentences and thoughts in perfect sync, like a duet singing in unison. Since then, we have developed a close working relationship, and I am grateful for the help and guidance that Christine has provided me.

Christine and I both believe that the education system requires reform. There is a significant gap between what is taught in schools and what children need to thrive. Unfortunately, there is a common belief that teacher and parent roles are separate and never meet. However, in a school setting, the teacher and parent must work together to ensure the child's optimal growth and development.

Our guiding mantra was, "It takes a village." We wanted to create a resource that could bring together caregivers, teachers, and students in a collaborative effort to improve education outcomes. This initiative gave birth to the movement #BridgingTheEducationalGap.

My colleague Christine and I are excited to take this work to the next level. We are creating parenting classes and professional development opportunities for teachers and parents that will provide practical strategies for working with each other. We aim to shrink the gap between home and school so that children can be more successful academically, socially, emotionally, and behaviorally. When teachers and caregivers form a united front, they can better support each child's unique needs and abilities, which benefits everyone involved.

Using this outside-of-the-box thinking, we could identify the lack of role responsibilities for parents, and teacher engagement was scarce, and we needed clarification. From there, we created a Venn Diagram framework that helps identify all the areas where children need help and support. The purpose of the Venn Diagram is to show the overwhelming areas where responsibilities overlap between home and school.

Each skill set has a more detailed list showing all included in learning that skill. For example, learning communication skills is more than just talking. It includes teaching your child to talk, listen, and ask for help. These skills are all topics that both teachers and caregivers are responsible for.

Living beyond boundaries offers the opportunity to discover one's true potential and to live a life filled with purpose and meaning. It involves a willingness to navigate ambiguity and find one's path, even when the road ahead seems uncertain. It is about embracing the complexity and diversity of life, breaking free from limiting beliefs, and exploring the vast possibilities beyond conventional norms. It requires a willingness to be curious, courageous, and open to new experiences, even in uncertainty.

Life's grey zone is a complex, dynamic space characterized by constant change and unpredictability. Living beyond boundaries in this space requires unique skills and qualities that enable individuals to navigate the challenges that arise. These qualities include resilience, adaptability, and the ability to thrive in constant change.

By embracing these complexities and uncertainties of life, we can break free from our limiting beliefs and explore the vast possibilities beyond conventional norms. It's about pushing beyond one's comfort zone, embracing the unknown, and understanding that growth and fulfillment are achieved by stepping beyond the boundaries of what is familiar and safe.

So, I challenge you to embrace this unconventional thought process and join us in our call to action to #Bridging the educational gap. Push yourself beyond boundaries. Know you can solve issues you feel morally strong about with tact and grace by presenting solutions to problems and asking others to join in on your mission and vision. When we join forces with others, great things can happen for years!

With 25 years of experience in Special Education, Kristin Lynne Nori is a highly skilled professional. She has a diverse skill set, including designing learning curricula, developing training programs, monitoring progress, analyzing data, and coaching other educators. Kristin specializes in special education, differentiation, inclusion and diversity, and children's and adults' social-emotional, behavioral, and mental health needs. She has successfully led school-wide programs for restorative practices, trauma-informed practices, and positive behavior intervention systems. Besides owning her business, Inclusion Advocates and Allies, LLC, as an Educational Advocate, Kristin is a National Professional Development Specialist and Coach for Catapult Learning. Along with her colleague, Kristin recently co-authored and published a guide for supporting parents with their child's education to help bridge the gap between home and school. She is eager for opportunities to collaborate in the future. norikristin728@gmail.com

To Aubrey & Emmett,

May you always shine bright, dream big, and work hard. Know I will always be in your corner and rooting for you both. I love you to infinity and beyond!

Love,

Aunt Kristin

Embracing the Marathon Towards True Success

By: Scott Raven

Hey y'all!

I'm Scott Raven and I live a wonderful life with my wife and kids in Atlanta. My story underscores not just overcoming obstacles, but transforming them into opportunities for growth. My journey embodies persistence, a commitment to authenticity, and the relentless pursuit of what matters most. Today, I'd like to share my story with you and how the lessons learned can be applied to your story and invitation to make your journey to success our story.

True success, as I've come to understand, isn't about reaching a final destination. It's a continuous journey of growth, learning, and realignment with our deepest values. It involves embracing our passions and ensuring our actions resonate with what we truly value. This path has reshaped my understanding of wealth—not just in financial terms, but as a wealth of purpose and well-being. This shift is crucial, especially for those feeling caught in the trade-off between time and money, often leading to a sense of isolation and unfulfillment.

This especially applies to men. According to a recent study, 1 in 6 adult men indicated they don't feel they have any true friends in their lives. If you're one of them, trust me, I've been there, and I'm here to share that there's a fulfilling way forward.

My experiences have produced a simple framework for navigating life's complexities: Aligning Your Power, Developing Your Plan, and Raising Your Game. This isn't merely about traditional success but redefining it to achieve fulfillment on your terms, which paves the way to Unleash Your Genius.

As we embark on this journey, consider these pivotal questions:

- Where are you headed?
- What drives you?
- How can you align your professional endeavors with your deeper purpose?

I invite you to join me, and together, we'll delve into aligning your passions with your daily actions, crafting a strategy that's both bold and deeply personal, and elevating your capabilities to levels you've only dreamed of. It's about creating a life story that resonates with courage, resilience, and fulfillment, ensuring every chapter reflects a step towards true success as defined by you.

But before we get to your story, which hopefully will become our story, let me share with you my story.

My Story

Growing up, I bought into the idea that a fat bank account was the ultimate scorecard of a life well-lived. Fast forward to my 40th birthday, and you would've thought I was living the dream. Picture this: a day out at the ballpark with my work crew, followed by a family dinner where my son managed to lose not one, but two baby teeth. It felt like I had hit the jackpot, measuring life by the size of my wallet.

Sounds like the perfect life, right?

As fate would have it, a storm was brewing just beyond the horizon, ready to test every belief I held dear.

The company I had been working for entered into a large, multi-billion-dollar merger with another firm, and there was a need to reduce expenses and gain synergies from the merger. To be frank, I did not handle the environment well because I didn't have the mental toughness to deal with all the shenanigans. But I also didn't get a lot of help either. Those who I had trusted in for many years were not acting in my best interest when I needed them the most.

Just like that, my executive position was eliminated, and I was out of a job.

The initial wave of relief from leaving the corporate battleground quickly turned into an aimless drift into the unknown. My identity had been so intertwined with my job that, stripped of that title, I found myself lost, a mere shadow of the man I once was. This loss plunged me into a deep, shadowy valley of depression and alcoholism. Lost without a clear direction and too ashamed to seek the help I desperately needed, I found myself spiraling uncontrollably toward rock bottom.

Everything came to a head just before Christmas of 2017. I picked the kids up from school and felt severe pains in my chest, head, and back. No one else saw anything visibly wrong with me, including my family, but I knew something was not right. As we returned to the house and were about to sit down for dinner, I pulled my wife aside and said I needed to go to the ER. In the ER, they immediately pulled me into the back room and took my blood pressure reading.

It was 180/110.

A flurry of tests confirmed it wasn't a heart attack or anything life-threatening, just severe hypertension. Yet, lying in that ER bed, awaiting admission for overnight observation, a profound fear gripped me. As my family, with my seven-year-old son's anxious eyes searching mine for reassurance, gathered around, I couldn't shake the thought: What if these were my final moments with them? What words of love and guidance would I leave my son with?

Such a thought is a chilling wake-up call, a moment I

wouldn't wish on anyone. Despite the turmoil within me, one truth remained crystal clear: I was a husband and dad first and foremost, determined to be the best dad possible for my children.

This resolve was deeply rooted in my own childhood. I grew up with a father who was a titan in his professional world but often couldn't be that close male figure in my world at home. Don't get me wrong – today, we're close and I love him for how he brings joy to my life and my family's life, especially my kids. But during that time, while he provided materially, he lacked the time to offer the emotional presence and guidance I yearned for.

Vowing to break this cycle, I promised to be a different kind of dad for my kids—one who was not only a provider but also a constant source of support and love.

Lying there, facing the stark reality of my health and life choices, I knew a profound change was imperative. It was time to redefine my priorities and embark on a journey to not only reclaim my health but also to fulfill my deepest commitment to being the dad my kids and my wife deserved.

My path to regaining my health and essence felt like a marathon. Very apropos as I had run actual marathons for a cause close to my heart – supporting cancer research with the Dana-Farber Cancer Institute. Just four months after my health scare, I ran the 2018 Boston Marathon, notoriously dubbed "the run through the washing machine" due to its brutal conditions. And I was still on my road to controlling my anxiety – if you've ever had pins and needles in your feet, think about that sensation randomly and without warning cropping up all over your body. But I stayed true to my resilience and perseverance to see my training through, and I proudly crossed the finish line that year in 4 hours, 49 minutes.

Reflecting on my fight of nature's fury that fateful day in April, I realized I was fighting a similar storm within, pushing past limits I hadn't known I could surpass. This battle rekindled a flame I thought I had lost forever – my sense of identity. And in the months that followed, that's exactly what I got back, ultimately allowing me to re-enter the workforce a changed and stronger man.

I thought my journey was over. In truth, it was merely the starting line of a much longer race.

The shadow of potential unemployment due to a reduction in force via multi-billion-dollar merger loomed again by the end of 2019. I had to make a choice: continue in the familiar corporate realm or carve a new path. Driven by a longing for change and to break free from a cycle that felt increasingly misaligned with my values, I chose the latter. Inspired by my son's enthusiasm for martial arts, I embraced entrepreneurship, diving into managing my own martial arts studios with a rapidly expanding franchise, and hoping to align my career with my passions.

This new venture was exhilarating, offering a fresh perspective far removed from my corporate past. As a small business owner on Main St., I relished the distinct challenges and rewards it brought. It also allowed me to interact with my customers, their parents, and my teammates in a way that was more authentic and not "corporate".

However, this endeavor eventually revealed a disconnect between the business model and my innate strengths. Relying on sheer willpower, a finite resource, led to an inevitable burnout. Acknowledging that my energies and time were not being utilized as they should, I made the tough but necessary decision to step away, regardless of the significant sunk costs, financially and emotionally.

I immersed myself in contemplation to reflect on everything that had occurred. I thought about the lessons the universe intended for me to learn through these events. Ultimately, I came to this realization: success isn't merely a destination but a vibrant journey of continuous growth, learning, and adjustment. It's about unveiling our inherent genius, embracing our passions fervently, and aligning our deeds with our deepest convictions.

Not only had I found the catalyst to my purpose, I had found my purpose itself – to share this wisdom with others.

I invested not just hard work and energy, but a rejuvenated passion that had been dormant for too long. Along the way, I was fortunate to connect with mentors and peers who genuinely supported my growth. Their encouragement and guidance were instrumental as I founded The Raven Group, aiming to illuminate this path of authentic success for others.

What I am today is something I know everyone can achieve because we all carry resilience in the human spirit. I'm here to tell you that life is more than just weathering life's storms; it's about moving to your beat, finding the bright side in every moment of your life (even the bad and crappy ones), and creating a legacy that surpasses traditional markers of success.

Your Story

I extend an invitation to you to ponder your own journey, knowing that I'm walking besides you in support. Consider where you're headed, what fuels your passion, and how you can align your professional life with your true calling. These pivotal inquiries have shaped my own journey, and I'm here to assist you in navigating yours. We'll delve into the foundations of success that have lit my way—embracing self-discovery, crafting a strategic vision, building essential skills, achieving balance, managing risks, and building a network. These pillars aren't mere concepts; they're practical tools and strategies designed to revolutionize your life and career, unlocking your full potential.

This transformative journey is about more than just wanting a different life; it demands a strategic approach that touches the core of our being, aiming towards who we aspire to become. It's a journey underpinned by three critical pillars: Aligning Your Power, Developing Your Plan, and Raising Your Game.

Aligning Your Power

Aligning Your Power is the bedrock of transformation. It's about peeling back the layers to reveal your core—discovering what truly drives you, your passions, and aligning them with your professional endeavors. This alignment is achieved by confronting the hard questions, those that cut to the heart of your identity and aspirations. It's in this clarity of vision where the true power lies, serving as the north star for your journey forward.

You can begin this journey yourself right here, right now. Find a sheet of paper and separate into four parts. Each part will be you responding to each of these questions in order:

- What are the dreams that you have for yourself, your

family / loved ones, and for you as a professional?

- Looking at your dreams, what are the doubts that you have that you feel may not allow these dreams to come true?
- Looking at your dreams, what are the drains – the time and energy vampires – that are preventing you from achieving your dreams.
- Finally, and this gets a bit into the next pillar, what do you intend to do to realize your dreams and push past your doubts and drains?

As you go through this exercise, I invite you to put this to what I call "the obituary test". The test is simple – if you were to pass away and someone else was to write the story of your life, would you be happy with how they'd speak of you? If as you do this you'd like a better story, go back to either your dreams or your do part and improve it to get to where you want to go.

Speaking of getting to where you want to go, that's a great lead into the next pillar, developing your plan.

Developing Your Plan

Developing Your Plan transitions vision into action. It's an audacious commitment to not only dream big but also to embrace the challenges that come with reaching beyond your current grasp. The essence of this pillar is the courage to chart a course towards goals that may seem daunting, armed with the conviction that they will be achieved. This plan isn't a rigid roadmap but a living document, adaptable and responsive to the growth and learning that unfold along the way.

Developing your plan requires a balance between strategy and tactics along with a desire to take action. The phrase "plan the work and work the plan" is critical here because there are many great plans that don't produce results because folks don't drive enough action. Oftentimes this shows up in the form of procrastination driven by an underlying self-fear, doubt, or negative belief from their past that they can't get past. Addressing these as they arise is critical to driving success, particularly when you don't feel you have the capability yet to do something.

Raising Your Game

That's where having the commitment and courage to try new things comes in, and ultimately the third pillar, raising your game. Raising Your Game encapsulates the essence of continuous improvement and strategic advancement. It's an invitation to level up your skills, to refine your strategies, and to surround yourself with a tribe that pushes you towards greatness. This pillar is about more than just personal development; it's about creating a synergy that elevates your entire being—professionally and personally. Raising your game is an ongoing journey of learning, adapting, and excelling in the face of life's myriad challenges.

In this transformative journey, you'll tap into depths of growth and potential that surpass your wildest expectations. But your actions will need to be bold:

- Commit to significant, transformative growth rather than settling for minor, incremental changes propels you further.
- Release the anchors of your past — be it people, places, or habits that chain you to your old self.
- Embrace change and dare to venture beyond the familiar is essential

Adopting these pillars of success isn't just about setting a course for achievement; it's about committing to a dynamic, evolving process of self-discovery and alignment. Challenges transform into opportunities to sharpen your vision, fortify your determination, and authenticate your existence both personally and professionally. This journey, unique and deeply personal, is not dictated by rigid rules but guided by insights and strategies designed to inspire and facilitate your path to a life filled with purpose, passion, and fulfillment. Thriving on your own terms, aligned with your truest essence and supported by a community that lifts you, you're not merely reaching for success; you're crafting a meaningful legacy and stepping into a more authentic, empowered, and fulfilled version of yourself.

Our Story

So now, I have a simple question for you: are you ready to take action and begin the journey to unleash your genius to achieve success on your terms?

To aid you on this path, I offer a free key focus areas assessment, designed to ignite the spark of self-discovery and to illuminate the strengths and passions that define your unique potential. Upon completing this assessment, I welcome the opportunity to connect with you for a personal chat. Together, we'll delve into your top focus area, drawing out at least one actionable insight that you can apply immediately to catalyze your growth. This is not just an assessment; it's the beginning of a conversation about who you are and who you aspire to be.

Wrapping this up, I circle back to an essential question: how will you chase your dreams, overcoming doubts and obstacles along the way? For me, it's about expanding my business to positively influence 10,000 lives in the next three years, bringing my family closer to our financial freedom goal. This journey towards purpose, wealth, and well-being doesn't mean sacrificing one for another. If you share this belief, I invite you to join me. By tapping into our collective genius, we're set to create a lasting legacy of success and positive change that echoes into the future.

Let's begin this adventure together.

Scott Raven is a transformative coach and entrepreneur, renowned for guiding individuals from corporate backgrounds to entrepreneurial success. With over twenty-five years of experience in corporate leadership as well as operating Main St. business locations, Scott transitioned to launch The Raven Group. His mission is to empower aspiring entrepreneurs and professionals to unleash their genius, crafting businesses that align with their passions and strengths. Through his unique coaching programs, Scott offers both private and group coaching, focusing on self-discovery, strategic planning, and execution excellence. His approach combines strategic insight with empathetic support, enabling clients to achieve wealth and well-being on their terms. Holding a BS in Computer Science from the University of Pennsylvania and an MBA from Carnegie Mellon University, Scott's expertise is underpinned by substantial academic and practical experience. Residing in Atlanta with his family, Scott is dedicated to creating a legacy of positive impact and personal fulfillment.

To my family – Kham, Asher, and Zoe – who through all the ups and downs are my constant true north, and are the catalyst behind my why in all that I pursue in life.

Walking Through Fire: Blazing the Path

By: Chanda Spates

As I sit here, penning down the tumultuous events that altered the course of my life and my son's, memories surge, overwhelming me with emotions akin to walking through fire. It was a period of relentless trials, where each day felt like navigating through a blazing inferno, yet I refused to succumb to the engulfing flames. Instead, I summoned the strength to brave the inferno, not just for my son but for every parent who might one day find themselves in a similar crucible.

The saga unfolded during what my son aptly termed a "three-Pete" – a trifecta of trauma that besieged us relentlessly. It began with my battle against breast cancer, culminating in a double lumpectomy, amidst the disintegration of my marriage. Concurrently, my son, born with cerebral palsy, faced his tribulations, exacerbated by a transition to high school where the shadows of bullying loomed ominously.

My son's indomitable spirit shone through from his early years despite the physical hurdles he encountered. Yet, as he traversed the corridors of North Charlotte High School, the relentless taunts and physical assaults dimmed the radiance in his eyes. What began as occasional teasing in middle school metamorphosed into a harrowing ordeal of daily torment – from verbal jibes to vicious beatings orchestrated by a multitude of assailants.

The school's response, characterized by a callous adherence to zero-tolerance policies, compounded our anguish. My son, the victim of relentless aggression, found himself punished with suspensions while his tormentors roamed free. The toll on his mental well-being was profound, plunging him

239

into the depths of depression and eroding his self-worth.

As I navigated the labyrinth of bureaucratic indifference, attending countless IEP meetings and legal hearings, the enormity of the systemic injustice weighed heavily upon me. The final blow came when faced with yet another suspension for self-defense, my son's despair reached a nadir, culminating in a desperate act of self-harm.

As I sat outside the ambulance, clutching onto hope amidst a maelstrom of anguish, a resolve crystallized within me. In that crucible of despair, I shed the cloak of passivity, embracing an unwavering commitment to champion the rights of the voiceless. No longer would I tolerate the callous disregard of vulnerable children by an indifferent system.

It was a decision that would lead me down unexpected paths, pushing me beyond my comfort zone and into the unknown. With each step I took, I felt a renewed sense of purpose, a flicker of hope that refused to be extinguished. And so, I forged ahead, determined to reclaim the happiness that had eluded me for so long.

But just as I began to find my footing, tragedy struck with a force that left me reeling. It started with whispers in the shadows, cruel taunts, and mocking laughter that echoed through my children's school halls. At first, I brushed it off as playful teasing, a harmless rite of passage that all children must endure. However, as the whispers grew louder and more menacing, I realized that it was anything but harmless.

In the transition from middle to high school, my son faced a relentless barrage of bullying. His unique way of walking, a result of cerebral palsy, made him an easy target. Every day, he endured taunts and physical assaults, with a total of nine kids ganging up against him at one point. In the most severe instance, an astonishing twenty-two assailants descended upon my child, who instigated nothing—no provocation other than trying his best to move.

To compound our agony, the school administration's response was appalling. Rather than protect the victim, they punished him, citing his "participation" in fights where he was the target. This twisted interpretation of a zero-tolerance policy exposed the systemic failure to address bullying and gang violence plaguing our schools.

As the nightmare unfolded, my son's dread of school grew, mirroring the despair felt by countless families in similar predicaments across our city. Frustrated by the lack of effective support, I searched for solutions. With suicide rates among teens skyrocketing nationwide, I refused to dwell on causes; I demanded actionable remedies to safeguard my child.

Balancing the responsibilities of a single mother amid personal health crises and legal battles, each day felt like navigating a minefield. Financial struggles forced me to donate blood just to put food on the table. The temptation to surrender loomed large, but I found the courage to fight back through prayer. Sharing my story ignited a movement, uniting parents, survivors, and advocates under a common cause.

I leveraged every opportunity to amplify our voices, challenging corporate leaders to join our crusade. Recognizing that conventional therapies often fell short with teens, I championed innovative approaches tailored to their needs. My mantra became: reject defeat, seek solutions, and when none exist, create them.

Throughout all that I did to fight for my son, encouraged him, prayed with and for him, and talked to him, I wasn't aware that he was in his own mind protecting me and to his detriment in not wanting to concern me. At the same time I battled my health crisis and multiple lumpectomy and reconstruction surgeries.

Our trifecta of traumatic events bombarding us was weighing on my son far too heavily for a child. Afraid to add more coals to the fiery path in which we walked, my son empathetically spared me the gory details of how bad the bullying had become.

He was afraid to tell some of the most unspeakable abuses that he endured, walking his own path through the fire within his school. Like so many adolescents and teens, his depression led to self-isolation and being away from family that may have been able to help.

Feeling hopeless as each bullying incident was met not with compassion, nor liberty and justice for all, instead was met with punishment-10 day unilateral suspensions for all, even the victim of bullying, thanks to the school's, in my opinion, ADA and certainly IDEA violating zero tolerance for fighting policy which disproportionately impacts the most vulnerable students with disabilities - a policy which that remains in place to this day.

Minds young and not yet fully developed with life experience, self-advocacy skills, and vernacular needed to navigate such challenges alone, my son and the 1.7 million other youth across the nation that attempt suicide each year, he also turned to suicide as a solution.

Thankfully, his cousin saw the social media post warning of his suicide attempt and alerted her mother, whom in turn alerted me.

I left work that day in absolute panic! I contacted 911 to send someone ahead of me to check on my him. EMS arrived. With no one answering the door, I permitted EMS to enter the home. Inside the upstairs bathroom, they found my son unresponsive. As I drove up to our driveway, viewing the ambulance in front of our home, they already had my son in the ambulance and attempted to revive him. I sat behind the vehicle, crying, screaming at the world, praying to God to save my baby, and vowing to do anything and everything that I could make a difference so that other moms and dads would never have to agonize in this way. I wouldn't wish this, not even on my enemy.

As we journeyed through the next year of counselors and tried to find mentors and positive male role models and programs for him, I found that resources were not easily accessible, especially for a single mom. Our nation's system offers FMLA time off yet unpaid time off to care for a child. Complex truths muddy the waters in finding solutions for kids. Counseling was offered, yet we found that statistics confirm that youth are notoriously non-compliant patients. Offering adult solutions such as traditional counseling simply isn't well received by children, who often report feeling stigmatized, reluctant to share with counselors, and have the highest rate of missed appointments as a result.

Having experience in corporate gap analysis, I researched research on what may work better to engage my son so that he could and, more importantly, he would, receive the support he desperately needed. When what he needed was not readily available and accessible -for various reasons, limited finances, insurance loopholes that allow for counseling yet effectively limit counseling beyond 6 sessions a year without further approval-approval that was denied by the insurance company physicians even though the need was documented by multiple doctors from the inpatient mental health facility that assessed him over a 72-hour hold and his counselor, yet three approvals were needed.

This insurance was useless for us, and I had to pay out of pocket for his visit until the next calendar year reset is 6 visit allotment. FMLA protected my job, yet my managers put pressure on me to use less time. His counseling appointments required a parent to bring the child to appointments, and the horrific divorce left our family alienated as we learned that to some, divorce means that the sole responsibility for children falls on the custodial parent-yet that's an entirely new degree to this fiery furnace life had become for us.

Unapologetic resolve to find or create solutions emerged from our nightmare of hurdles, storms, and fires. This turning point came when I grew weary of systemic failures and the lack of youth-focused programs and counseling. Recognizing that silence only breeds isolation and acceptance of the unacceptable, I resolved to speak out. Through social media, I connected with thousands who shared similar experiences, realizing our collective strength in unity.

This catalyst moment was one of new boldness and resolve to simply not take no for an answer. I resolved to no longer be silent and to build a dynamic network of people and organizations that are heart-centered and committed to creating solutions.

Telling my story has led to the events listed below, including the nation's first citywide initiative for suicide prevention, the creation of programs such as after-school programs, mentoring and counseling programs, and a music and mental resilience campaign. This initiative unites music industry professionals and technology companies to create highly engaging programs addressing teens where they are – in their music. Young people ages 13-26 spend more than 3-5 hours combined consuming music and video content. Teaching youth to make a dent in the national suicide crisis requires engaging them in ways they embrace. Today, by telling my family's story and campaigning across the nation's professional social media spaces, and engaging corporations to encourage social responsibility, I've managed to create a powerful army of volunteers and more than 125 collaborative organizations united through memorandums of understanding (MOUs) to do more than talk. United through the collective commitment to create and implement programs that help create safe and caring communities and schools and address the alarming national suicide crisis among teens and young adults together. Today, I stand before you no longer as a lone mom on a mission, but as a testament that one person's voice can start a ripple effect that begins a national movement.

Today, as the Flourish Foundation Project, doing business as DDAAT-App!™ National Suicide & School Safety Coalition, we are working tirelessly to save a generation from suicide. We are working to save our children, your children, and all children. We unapologetically forge forward to save our nation's youth; we simply can't wait for someone else to make the necessary change .

My passion is building a dynamic network for teen suicide prevention, safe, caring schools, and communities. As the founder of DDAAT-App! National Suicide Prevention & School Safety Coalition, my mission is to create and implement collaborative mental health solutions for social impact city by city!

We facilitate catalytic movements for social impact by merging visionary missions, technology, and community engagement. By uniting businesses, community leaders, educational institutions, and mental health organizations, we can improve access to and the effectiveness of suicide prevention efforts within our communities.

Our organizational missing stems from my personal experiences, where I've leveraged corporate know-how to create mobile research-based social impact applications. We empower youth through STEM, Art, Music, and more.

We produce music that matters, gamified solutions, and educational workshops and events that train youth to become ambassadors in their schools, helping to recognize & prevent crises by alerting responsible adults. We help youth find the voice of self-advocacy and instill mental resiliency and civic responsibility that help our schools and communities thrive.

In the last year, we've made strides in bringing this technology nationwide, securing commitments from businesses, mental health agencies, celebrities, athletes, an NFL team, and three universities ready to validate our program. This local program holds national impact potential, as the interventions can be streamed to schools, colleges, and universities nationwide via our youth-run peer support channel.

Our program introduces groundbreaking features:

- First and the original citywide behavioral intervention addressing teen & young adult suicide
- Single sign-on Mobile Access Hub to community suicide prevention resources
- An upcoming gamified solution for proactive school safety, Mental Resilience, and emergency preparedness training packaged and designed specifically for today's youth!

Not in 1000 years would I have imagined that I'd build such an undertaking, yet through my family's pain, I have found purpose, strength, and the daring ability to forge and blaze a path for others. My life has a purpose that wakes me up daily, ready to create new solutions and connections that impact our kids profoundly and daily.

In 2023, our nation witnessed the highest number of suicides and mass shootings in recorded history. 2024 is unfortunately off to the races, and Collaboration is essential to making an impact. We need your support to save lives and create safer communities.

I urge you to share your story, defy obstacles, and unite with others to forge solutions. Let your pain guide you to your purpose. My traumatic journey led me to advocate for change, and yours can, too.

Acknowledging that traditional counseling methods often fall short with youth is crucial. Many young people reject talking to a stranger on a couch, leading to high rates of missed appointments—a concern for both parents and therapists. My mission became clear: to create engaging solutions that meet youth where they are, elevating them toward mental resiliency.

Looking back on the journey, I realize that every trial and tribulation was a stepping stone towards my greater purpose. The pain and adversity I endured were not in vain; they were the catalysts for change and the fuel that propelled me forward. Today, I stand as a beacon of hope, a testament to the power of resilience, and a living example that no obstacle is insurmountable when faced with unwavering determination and an unapologetic commitment to change the world for the better.

I've learned that through the flames of my darkest moments, I've witnessed my transformational evolution from brokenness into a woman determined to defy all odds. I've learned and hope that my story has empowered you also to find your unapologetic voice of purpose and change. Each trial and setback becomes a stepping stone on the path to unimaginable success for true social impact. May my story be a testament to the power of perseverance, a beacon of hope for those walking through their fiery path of trials and tribulations who emerge empowered to blaze a path for others in their own way.

The challenges I faced were myriad, from personal medical crises to navigating the unfamiliar terrain of single parenting following a divorce, all while seeking solutions for my child. Many times, these challenges felt unbearable, like walking through fire, as my son aptly described the tumultuous period in our lives. After enduring the weight of these struggles alone, the silent anguish weighed heavily. Moreover, fighting against the desperate impact of zero-tolerance policies on disabled children and struggling to be heard added layers of difficulty.

From this story of resilience, remember three key points: first, silence only leaves us isolated and powerless; second, adversity can be overcome through perseverance and a solution-focused mindset; and finally, our journey through hardship lights the way for others, inspiring them to navigate their own challenges with courage and determination. Let us remember that by sharing our stories and standing up against adversity, we not only find strength within ourselves but also illuminate the path for others to follow.

Chanda Spates, a trailblazing Mom-on-a-Mission and advocate for suicide prevention, leads FICE-Apps, Inc. (Flourish Individual & Community Empowerment) and Flourish Foundation Project Inc DBA DDAAT-App! (TM) National Suicide Prevention & School Safety Coalition. Motivated by personal adversity—her son's suicide attempt resulting from extreme bullying by a gang in his school targeting him due to his cerebral palsy-induced limp—Chanda is on a mission to create safe & caring schools and communities nation Her commitment to suicide prevention and school safety is evident through initiatives like DDAAT-App! and Music & Mental Resilience, which have gained global recognition. These initiatives integrate behavioral science, technology, STEMM+ Music, leadership, and civic responsibility, recognizing that youth spend an average of 3-5 hours daily consuming music and videos. With a Master's in Human Resources Management, she has leveraged her HR and gap analysis skills to develop a comprehensive national suicide prevention model. Through over 12 years of experience in Corporate Training & Development and high-impact performance training, she has strategically forged collaborative initiatives that foster safe and caring communities and schools. Learn more & connect at www.ddaat-app.com, www.FICE-apps.com, and www.flourish.foundation or FB/IG @ddaatapp.Instagram

Strength of A Mother's Love
To save my child, I'd change the entire world.
-Chanda Linell Spates

Dedicated to those feeling overwhelmed and underestimated, may you muster the courage to push back unapologetically. To my son, whose unwavering resilience lights up my days. Your strength is a beacon of inspiration, surpassing even your awareness. To my children, who are my reason to move mountains with all my heart and soul. To my father, whose strength knows no bounds. To my brothers, sisters-in-law, nieces, and nephews, with endless love.

In loving memory of my mother and sister, Linell Brewington and Melinda Cashel Brewington-DeMons

Special thanks to Dr. Constance Leyland for the opportunity to be included in the anthology book. This is an amazing project.

From Adversity to Empowerment: A Journey of Resilience and Purpose

By: Dr. Nhu Truong

Have you ever found yourself grappling with life's greatest questions? Every obstacle, from youthful curiosity to battles against ingrained societal prejudices and through the echoes of personal loss, has relentlessly tested the very foundation of my resilience. From a tender age, a persistent whisper has haunted my thoughts: "What is life truly for?" Surely, our journey cannot merely be confined to the monotonous rhythm of birth, toil, kinship, decay, and ultimately, the shroud of death. Such a stark cycle belies the profound richness that this ephemeral life teases, a seeming mockery of our treasured consciousness.

It was as if the circle of life that I envisioned was missing vital pieces, leaving me yearning for something more profound, something beyond the ordinary. I refused to accept that life was merely about following a predetermined cycle of events without purpose or significance.

As a child, I was at odds with societal norms, questioning why I felt different from those around me. Even the simplest tasks, like eating meat, became a battleground of conflicting emotions. While others savored the meal, I meticulously picked out every piece, unable to reconcile my distaste with societal expectations of gratitude.

Another quite ironic childhood memory was how I couldn't swallow pills. I would often gag on them, trying desperately to get them down with lots of water but failing to take the medicine. Even when I pleaded to drink it so I could feel better, or when I faced punishment and threats of a timeout if I didn't swallow them, I couldn't manage it. However, now I teach and help people take their medicine. I couldn't have imagined having a career as a pharmacist back then. Nonetheless, I always dreamed of becoming either a doctor or a teacher, aspiring to help and educate others through mentorship.

Arriving in the US, I faced numerous challenges: no English, little understanding of the culture, and no money. With only my immediate family — my father, mother, brother, and sisters — I felt like the odd one, often teased by classmates and teachers. To keep up with school, I had to teach myself and translate homework from English to Vietnamese, which took hours. Sacrificing social time, I focused solely on studying.

Tragically, my father passed away shortly after our arrival. He had been a captain in the Military Police during the Vietnam War. His sudden diagnosis of liver cancer after kidney stone surgery shocked us all. Despite suspicions of medical errors, we lacked the resources to challenge the system. That was the first indication that my purpose was to go into healthcare and provide better care for my loved ones.

Watching my mother shoulder the burden of single parenthood in a new country filled me with a profound sense of determination. Despite the absence of parental attendance at my performances and ceremonies, I remained laser-focused on making my parents proud, honoring their sacrifices with every achievement. They sacrificed everything for us to have better opportunities, freedom of speech, and the American dream. I was determined to make them proud.

Another adversity I faced was going through a hostage situation that nearly cost me my life. During that ordeal, I pleaded with the captor to release everyone else and keep only me. I knew that many people at the shop were parents with children, while I had no family or kids then. Some questioned why I would risk myself instead of prioritizing my safety.

However, looking back, I realize that I was meant to be there to help others because my true calling is to alleviate suffering and bring peace to people's lives.

Reflecting on the situation, I attribute my survival to my compassionate heart and empathy for others' pain. I couldn't help but think about the lasting effects on the captor and the immense pain they must have been experiencing to resort to such drastic actions. Despite the danger I faced, I genuinely cared for their well-being. I am grateful for the SWAT team and the police officers who were present that night and ensured our safety.

As I write this, I want to extend my forgiveness to the captor, their family, and all involved. I wish them peace and happiness, hoping they find solace and are not haunted by their experiences. Let us strive to spread more love, kindness, empathy, and compassion to one another. Everything happens for a reason, and it occurs to us for a specific purpose. Let's choose love and kindness for ourselves and others.

Reflecting on the current state of the world amidst times of war, widespread violence, and numerous mass shootings, it's evident that social media often amplifies negative stories. It perpetuates division rather than fosters unity. Now, more than ever, we need to cultivate love, kindness, empathy, and compassion for one another.

If we approach every individual respectfully and demonstrate genuine care without ulterior motives, viewing each person as part of our extended family, we could mitigate violence. The key to unifying humanity lies in leading with love, kindness, empathy, and compassion for all, irrespective of gender, financial status, culture, or religion. We must embody the change we wish to see in the world.

During my graduate pharmacy school, I tackled an accelerated 3-year program at MCPHS in Worcester, away from family and amidst a demanding curriculum. The school was notorious for its difficulty, with many students failing to finish. I also faced challenges with a preceptor rumored to be biased against non-Caucasian students, especially Asians. Despite this, I approached the situation with respect, completing tasks diligently. Over time, my consistent approach shifted my preceptor's perspective, earning her trust and respect. By the end of my rotation, she acknowledged my efforts, praising me as a standout student and awarding commendable grades, a significant achievement given the challenges faced by many students during her rotation.

Another significant challenge arose during my pharmacy school journey, which shook me to my core. It began with the devastating news of my mother's cancer diagnosis, followed closely by the news that my younger sister had been airlifted to the hospital after a car accident. She had crashed into an electric pole and was in a coma. My family chose to shield me from this information until a friend of my sister called me, inquiring about her well-being.

Initially unaware of the accident, I reassured the caller that my sister was fine, as I had spoken to my mother earlier. However, upon contacting my mother again and pressing her for details about my sister's condition, I learned about the severity of the incident. She had suffered a seizure while driving, which led to the crash.

I felt torn between returning home to support my family and continuing my pharmacy education. It was made more difficult when considering the significant financial investment I had already made. Despite the immense pressure, my family encouraged me to stay in school, ensuring they would keep me informed of my sister's progress and any need for my presence.

It was an incredibly challenging period for me—juggling academic demands, financial concerns, and the emotional turmoil of worrying about my family's well-being. I feared the additional burden my failure to complete the program successfully would place on my family. Every day, I struggled to maintain focus on my studies while constantly checking in on my sister's condition.

During this tumultuous time, my community's unwavering support and prayers sustained me, helping me navigate through one of the toughest chapters of my life. As I reflect, the options were clear: give up; put a pause on my efforts, and perhaps to try again later; or, to keep pushing forward despite the challenges. The last option meant finding the willpower to make it work, no matter what, even if it meant staying up all night studying for the exam while dealing with distractions and crashing afterward. I was determined not to give up, especially knowing my sister was fighting for her life.

I recall a teacher telling me I wouldn't pass my board exam. Reflecting on that moment, I realized that passing the exam required intense preparation and absorbing vast information. The feedback from those who doubted me only strengthened my determination to prove myself through hard work and sacrifice. I had to sacrifice social gatherings while managing numerous responsibilities, but giving up was never an option. With my strong mindset, work ethic, dedication, and prayers, I was committed to succeeding. As a result, I passed my board exam on the first attempt, proving my determination and resilience.

I used to think that achieving success in my life meant overcoming racism, immigrant challenges, earning a doctorate degree, and establishing a thriving career. However, as I progressed through various career paths and assumed leadership positions post-graduation, I came to realize that true fulfillment came from making a positive impact on the lives of others.

In my leadership and hiring roles, I strived to offer opportunities to individuals who lacked traditional qualifications but demonstrated strong moral and ethical principles. I invested in their growth within the company by providing training and employment. Being a minority gave me a unique perspective, allowing me to empathize with others facing diverse struggles on their path to success.

Although my career may have seemed successful from the outside, few knew about the sacrifices I made, including countless unpaid hours and time away from my family. I was consistently searching for innovative solutions to enhance team dynamics and address challenges, always placing the well-being of others above financial gain. I firmly believe that by serving, supporting, and empowering others, financial success naturally follows.

I aspire to make a positive difference in my family's life and the lives of many others. Despite this desire, I've often felt that my efforts fell short of expressing enough gratitude for their love, support, and sacrifices. Internally, I struggled with a sense of inadequacy, feeling that my actions didn't measure up to the immense sacrifices my family made by leaving their homeland for better opportunities for us children. There seemed to be a gap, a need for external validation to recognize my achievements, especially since we were all occupied with the demands of everyday life. Whether influenced by our Asian culture or family dynamics, we rarely celebrated accomplishments. My achievements often went unnoticed amidst my mother's challenges as a working parent and our family's journey through life's obstacles. My struggle wasn't about how others perceived me but rather my battle with self-belief and the quest to create a more meaningful impact.

Another difficulty emerged in my career when I faced the decision of conforming to the flawed system or speaking up to establish processes that could prevent individuals from enduring abuse at the hands of their managers or organization bosses and owners. Drawing from firsthand experience in navigating a toxic work environment, I understood the potential consequences, as it could lead someone to contemplate self-harm or harm others.

Our choices are ours to live with, and it's a decision that carries its weight on our conscience. I soon found myself in the midst of the most challenging period of my life, filled with continuous tests and obstacles. From financial hardships to grieving the loss of my nephew and navigating one after another health crises, I had to make decisions. My options were to either prioritize working for financial stability or make sacrifices for our family's mental well-being and balance, ensuring I could be present for my two small children who needed my attention.

I resigned and walked away from a toxic workplace that wasn't truly focused on serving people, despite it's a wellness place in the healthcare sector. Witnessing that unveiled another harsh reality of our society, where many wear masks and prioritize profit over human lives. I was shocked to realize how the healthcare industry, which should inherently prioritize care, could be so indifferent to one another.

It was difficult to decide to leave such a negative environment, regardless of my efforts to make a positive impact. I learned that you cannot change someone unwilling to change themselves. Despite my efforts and earnest wishes for transformation, I understood how people need to awaken to the importance of treating others with dignity and respect.

Though leaving behind colleagues and patients I deeply cared for was tough, I also recognized that I had a choice. I could either contribute to a cycle of negativity or channel my energy into raising awareness about treating each other as fellow human beings, not mere statistics. It was the moment I stood up for what's right and amplified the voices of those who lacked the courage to speak up. It was a reminder that true success is measured not by material wealth or accolades but by the impact we make in the lives of others.

I used to ponder, "Who am I to inspire others like Tony Robbins? I'm just an ordinary person." Yet, as I summoned the courage to share my stories, I discovered that people resonated with them, feeling seen and heard. Through collaborative writing projects, keynote speeches, and podcast appearances, I received messages from individuals whose lives my stories had touched. They found strength in navigating their own challenges, inspired by my journey. It was heartening to realize that our stories have the power to save lives and make a difference. These experiences showed me that my community, spanning the globe, valued my insights and experiences, prompting others to seek guidance on navigating life's adversities.

As I recount my tales of adversity and triumph, I reflect on how these challenges have molded me into who I am today. It all began with a simple desire — to lend a helping hand and amplify my voice to reach as many souls as possible. From that spark emerged the decision to launch my own business, dedicated to aiding individuals in their career and business journeys, sparking a ripple effect of support and empowerment.

My advice to those laboring under the banner of another's enterprise is simple yet profound: approach your work as if it were your own. By recognizing the intrinsic value of every individual and embracing them as part of your extended family, you sow the seeds for collective success and fulfillment.

Imagine the profound impact of saving a life or helping someone reclaim control over their destiny. Free of expectation, these selfless endeavors led me on an unexpected journey — speaking at international events, collaborating with diverse communities, and uncovering boundless opportunities to serve others.

Recognition as one of the top 50 influential pharmacy leaders in 2023 by the Pharmacy Podcast Network stands as a testament to the power of resilience and unwavering dedication to the cause of helping and uplifting others.

My purpose in sharing this journey is to inspire and empower you. If I can overcome adversity and achieve my dreams, so can you. Remember your why, values, and purpose, and let them guide you through the darkest moments toward success.

Along the way, extend a helping hand to others. We are stronger, and we can create positive change in the world by supporting one another. Your adversity is not a weakness but your superpower — a unique aspect of who you are.

Embrace your uniqueness, believe in yourself, and know you can overcome any obstacle. Be mindful of the power inherent in your thoughts and words, for they possess the capacity to shape your destiny and influence the world around you.

Remember, you are not alone on this journey. You can shape your destiny and create a future filled with hope and possibility. Keep pushing forward, stay true to yourself, and never forget: you've got this.

When life knocks you down, remember that it shall pass. Pay attention to the messages and lessons it brings. You learn a lot about yourself and others by being present and serving others.

In life's journey, we often question our purpose, face adversities, and navigate challenging situations. Reflecting on my own path, I've encountered moments of doubt, adversity, and uncertainty. Yet, in the face of adversity, I've discovered resilience, compassion, and the power of unwavering determination. Embrace your struggles as catalysts for personal growth and opportunities to make a positive impact in the lives of others.

Let us choose love, kindness, and empathy as guiding principles. Together, let us rise above the boundaries that seek to divide us, embracing our shared humanity and collective potential to create a brighter, more compassionate world. The journey of life is not merely about surviving but thriving — beyond boundaries, towards a future filled with hope, compassion, and endless possibilities to make a positive impact for generations to come.

Dr. Nhu Truong, recognized as one of the top 50 pharmacy leaders by the Pharmacy Podcast Network in 2023, brings over 13 years of experience as a Clinical Pharmacist. Inspired by mindfulness and meditation, Dr. Truong takes a holistic approach as an advocate, mentor, and business partner. She is committed to supporting the well-being of pharmacists and healthcare professionals, guiding them through challenges to rediscover joy and purpose in their lives. Dr. Truong invites you to embark on a transformative journey toward happiness, wellness, and success. Through her guidance, infused with mindfulness and compassion, she empowers you to unlock your potential and embrace positivity. Reach out to her to explore empowerment, mindfulness, and purpose in your life. Additionally, Dr. Truong is available for motivational keynote speaking engagements. Connect with her on LinkedIn or KN Health Consulting and follow her on YouTube.

LinkedIn: https://www.linkedin.com/in/dr-nhu-truong/
Website: knhealthconsulting.com. YouTube: @Dr.NhuTruongMindfulness

My commitment to my family, whose unwavering belief and support propel me forward, and to the pharmacy profession, remains steadfast. It is rooted in upholding values and purpose and treating patients as cherished members of our extended family, whether they are close by or far away. Let us unite in forging a path toward positively impacting our world. As one ranked among the top 50 most influential pharmacy leaders, I am fully aware of the responsibility that comes with this recognition. Beyond merely offering encouragement, I am responsible for leading by example and providing guidance and inspiration every step of the way. With unwavering dedication and determination, we can transform lives and carve out a brighter future for all

I wholeheartedly believe in each of you, empowering you to lead joyous, fulfilling lives filled with love for your pursuits. You've got what it takes!

Shades of Transformation: My Journey from Pharmacist to Holistic Entrepreneur

By: Jackie Lyn Velasco

"In the bustling world of healthcare, I found myself trapped in a grey zone - a space between what was comfortable and what my soul yearned for."

"And in that moment, I knew I had a higher calling. I wanted to empower my patients to take charge of their health and well-being, to guide them toward a path of true healing and thriving. I understood that there was a grey zone between the strict boundaries of my profession and the untapped potential for a holistic approach to healthcare. It was within this grey zone that my true purpose lay. I was meant for something more, something that would allow me to profoundly impact the lives of those I serve."

I am a pharmacist, and as a pharmacist, who currently works in a community pharmacy, I have spent countless hours counting pills, ensuring accurate prescriptions, giving vaccinations, and counseling patients about their medications. I love my work, as it gives me the opportunity to help someone each day. What I love about it is that I get to talk to people, understand their health issues, and be a part of the solution by providing them with the medication or medications to alleviate their symptoms, treat their infections, or manage their chronic diseases.

Becoming a pharmacist was my childhood dream. I wanted to become a pharmacist because my understanding then when I was about 10 years old, was that pharmacists make medicines to cure people who are sick *(which meant for me then- the people who have cancer or terminal illness)*. That understanding stuck with me, and I did not look to be in any other profession but to become a pharmacist, so I did. I have worked in various fields of pharmacy, from sales and marketing and manufacturing pharmaceuticals to hospital outpatient settings in oncology, academia, and now in the community setting, shifting from one area to another depending on the opportunity and the circumstances in life. I also had the opportunity to train other pharmacists and new students to become pharmacists, which I greatly enjoyed.

Working in the pharmacy field for many years has given me a sense of accomplishment and allowed me to excel in my profession and provide for my family. Through dedication, continuous learning, and a commitment to delivering high-quality care, I have developed skills and expertise that have contributed significantly to my success in solving the health needs of those I serve.

As a current practicing community pharmacist in a country big in healthcare, I have always understood the importance of following standards and conforming to the expectations of my profession. From ensuring accurate medication dispensing to counseling patients on potential side effects and drug interactions, my role has been defined by these responsibilities. I perform my role and carry out my responsibilities with the patient's best interest in mind. I provide an exceptional level of care that my patients appreciate greatly. I often give additional recommendations to support my patients' well-being, such as suggesting certain supplements to alleviate medication side effects or support their actions.

I sometimes inquire about the dietary habits of my patients who are diabetic or taking certain medications, as it is crucial to be aware that many medications have food and drug interactions that can have adverse effects. Frequently, the simple inquiry of "How are they doing?" holds profound significance for them. This question arises from remembering significant events such as surgeries, a child's bout of pneumonia, a past hospitalization due to an accident, or simply from remembering what medications they have had. This gesture of showing genuine concern and care for their welfare is deeply valued by my patients. It is met with appreciation and positive responses upon their return visits, as they often express how the extra attention, care, or time I have imparted has positively impacted their health. I believe it is these personalized interactions that create the most impact on my patients' well-being, together with providing the appropriate medication therapy.

I have always enjoyed this part of my work; however, as the years went by, I could not help but feel a sense of monotony and emptiness creeping into my daily routine, not to mention the thought of the increasing prevalence of sickness despite medical progress, experiencing the COVID-19 pandemic, why chronic diseases are on the rise, and why cancers are now occurring at younger ages?

One day, the realization hit me hard as I observed my patients' outcomes. It seemed as if many were merely being prescribed one medication after another, not truly healing or flourishing. I saw people relying solely on prescriptions to manage their health issues rather than actively taking control of their health and well-being. It is disheartening to witness their dependence on medication without any conscious understanding of how to improve their overall health and well-being.

It was at this moment; I knew I had a higher calling. I wanted to empower others to take charge of their health and well-being, to guide them toward a path of true healing and thriving. At this moment in my life, I decided to venture into entrepreneurship, a pivotal moment driven by a deep calling to help others beyond the limitations of my current title and pharmaceuticals. I have witnessed firsthand the struggles and frustrations of many individuals battling illnesses, desperately seeking other means to improve their health and overall well-being. This passion, my background in healthcare, and my belief in the power of nutrition and wellness practices propelled me toward this new journey.

As I took the initial steps toward establishing my business, fear began to grip me tightly. The comfort of the familiar, the security of a stable job, the amount of time, work, and money I had to put in seemed to hold me back. What if I failed? What if my aspirations were too ambitious? Doubts flooded my mind, clouding my vision and causing me to question my abilities. These uncertainties felt like a heavy load on my shoulders as if they were ready to squish my dreams before they could even start. The fear of not making it, of not living up to what I hoped for, kept nibbling at my confidence.

Yet, amidst the doubts and fear, a persistent voice within me refused to be silenced. It reminded me of the countless people whose lives could be transformed through the alternative or complementary wellness solutions I aimed to provide. It reminded me of the potential impact I could make and the unwavering belief I had in the power of natural healing that I experienced for myself when I was once faced with a health struggle at a young age.

A few years ago, I was diagnosed with a lump in my throat. I was devastated by the news. It has shaken me to the core, and I could not believe what I had just heard. As a mother of three young kids, it was a time in my life when I was so scared, not just for myself but for my loved ones. "What if it is cancer? What if I pass away?" I thought about my kids and my loving husband. How would they survive without me? The thought of leaving them behind was devastating. I was angry about what was happening then, so I joined a fitness competition out of rebellion and frustration. Little did I know, that I would be saved by exploring nutrition, exercise, and holistic wellness techniques, which I was obligated to follow as part of the preparation for this fitness contest. It was the changes that I made in my diet and the new lifestyle that I adopted that helped me manage and overcome this condition without even realizing it until later. A few months went by and my lump disappeared, and I did not have to undergo surgery or any other medical treatment. The stressors of that period, including the unhealthy diet I unconsciously consumed, likely contributed to its onset. But through healthy nutrition, wellness practices, and self-care, I survived and thrived.

Overcoming this health problem has served as an inspiration to help others who may experience the same. With this desire to help and empower others to take control of their health and see them heal and thrive, I made a choice. I embraced the discomfort, stepped outside my comfort zone, broke those barriers, and confronted my fears head-on. I realized that proper growth and fulfillment lie on the other side of fear, and it was time to push through.

I began by expanding my knowledge beyond the confines of traditional pharmacy education. I delved into nutrition, understanding that food is medicine, exercise, mindfulness, and alternative therapies. I have taken courses in fields like functional medicine from the **Institute for Functional Medicine (IFM)**, Pharmacogenomics, and Nutrigenomics from **ASHP**, and **Stanford** online to deepen my understanding of the relationship between nutrition and the root cause of many chronic diseases, including cancer. I have become a certified Health and Nutrition Life Coach, which has helped me gain confidence in encouraging clients to take action.

I continuously enhance my knowledge and expertise. I am currently taking classes to become an Oncology Nutrition consultant from the **Oncology Nutrition Institute (ONI)** to specialize and strengthen my cancer nutrition skills. I have explored yoga and meditation classes, which have helped me tremendously and have become part of the tools I share with clients. I have read hundreds of books about business, and self-development to equip me with business skills and to help me become a better entrepreneur. Among my favorites are **Think and Grow Rich** by Napoleon Hill, **The Seven Habits of Highly Effective People** by Stephen Covey, and **The Secret** by Rhonda Byrne. I sought out experts in various fields, taking their courses and attending seminars and conferences, eager to absorb their wisdom and gain a deeper understanding of the interconnectedness of all aspects of health. During these times, I also find myself having fun the most. I love learning new things and sharing what I have learned. It excites me to know that I will be armed with more tools to help provide the best solutions to my clients.

Empowered by this fresh understanding, I aimed to continuously adopt a holistic approach to my everyday routine, recognizing the importance of practicing what I preach. I began journaling every day, allotting time for meditation and exercise. I became more conscious of preparing nutritious home-cooked dishes and enjoyed meal planning for me and my family. I am committed to living in alignment with the principles I aim to impart.

Embracing the ambiguity of this transitional phase, I move forward with courage, determined not only to endure but to flourish. I anticipate challenges, particularly the initial resistance to unconventional methodologies, as many people are skeptical about moving away from traditional beliefs. However, I am confident that with the compelling evidence of positive transformations in the lives of many who have traveled this path, including myself, the concept of taking conscious responsibility for one's health and well-being will be the future standard of care.

Armed with a mission and a vision, a network of supportive individuals, and a relentless determination, Purple Nutrition and Wellness was born whose mission *is to empower individuals to make positive lifestyle choices that enhance their overall well-being and strive to be a trusted partner in our client's health journeys, providing them with the tools, knowledge, and support they need to lead healthy, vibrant lives.*

In this grey zone, we call life, I understood that failure should not be dreaded; instead, it is an opportunity for personal growth and learning. Thriving in the grey zone led me to the path of entrepreneurship. Entrepreneurship is not for the faint of heart. It requires resilience, perseverance, and an unwavering belief in oneself. It is within these moments of doubt and fear that true transformation occurs. When we confront our fears and push beyond our boundaries, we discover our true potential.

As I journey forward, the realization of my impact grows clearer. Each step is about personal growth and the profound intersection of personal development and entrepreneurship. With gratitude, resilience, and adaptability as my compass, I navigate the grey zone, where boundaries blur and possibilities flourish. Whether smooth or challenging, every moment contributes to my evolution as a holistic entrepreneur. By embracing uncertainties and imperfections, I transform setbacks into stepping stones, recognizing their potential to sculpt my character and deepen my understanding. My commitment is to survive and thrive, making meaningful connections and leaving a lasting legacy through Purple Nutrition and Wellness.

I want to thank you for taking the time to read my story and I hope that it has inspired you to transform challenges into opportunities and take charge of your health and wellbeing. If you resonate with my journey and feel that I can help empower you to live a healthier and happier life, please do not hesitate to reach out. I am more than happy to lend a helping hand and support you on your path to wellness. Remember, your health is precious and it is never too late to make positive changes. Together, we can create a life filled with more time spent with loved ones and moments of joy and fulfillment.

About Jackie Lyn Velasco, MS RPh

Ms. Jackie Lyn Velasco is a pharmacist, best-selling author, educator, wellness coach, and entrepreneur. With her unwavering dedication to improving the lives of others, she has become a beacon of hope for many individuals seeking to enhance their well-being.

With her extensive knowledge and expertise as a pharmacist, Jackie has made it her life's work to empower individuals to take a proactive approach to their health and well-being, which led to the launching of **Purple Nutrition and Wellness**™, a platform that bridges the gap between traditional medicine and holistic approaches utilizing cancer prevention strategies.

"Wellness is the foundation upon which we build our dreams. The cornerstone of our highest potential. Without it, our ability to serve and help others is limited. Let us prioritize our well-being, for in nurturing ourselves, we empower the world around us."
-Jackie Lyn Velasco
www.purplenutritionandwellness.com
jackie@purplenutritionandwellness.com
FB/IG/LI: @purplenutritionandwellness
FB/IG/LI: @jackievelascorph

Dedication

To my loving family,

You are my beacon of life and my greatest inspiration. Your unwavering support and love have been the driving force behind everything I do. Thank you for being my reason, and my greatest motivation to thrive. This book is dedicated to you, with all my love and gratitude.

Forever and always,

Mommyo (Jackie)

Curiosity Didn't Kill This Cat

By: Kinga Vajda

"Do you know *your* fractions?"

"I'm...not... sure," I said with shame.

The neighbor kid laughed at me. I probably understood basic algebra at the time. We were *'doing'* fractions years ago in class. I rarely missed school. How was I excluded when they assigned fractions out to everyone? Why did everyone else have *'their'* fractions? They must have owned something that I didn't. I was missing out.

I was different. They were all clued into something bigger. Meanwhile, I understood not only math but also language on a deeper level. I was literal and purposeful, so that possessive pronoun *'your'* really threw me off. I learned Hungarian and English at the same time growing up. Translations began so early in life.

Children of immigrant parents think and interpret concepts in different ways. The cultures we are raised in, our relationships with family, the world around us, and who we are can greatly conflict with what we see in society. My problem? I looked like everyone else. So, I felt hidden and in disguise. I felt society's pressure to pretend I was something I wasn't a nine-year-old imposter.

As a child of the '80s, I was never taught to honor my strengths as a curious person about human connection, self-growth, and impact. My father was an engineer, and I felt there was only one obvious choice for college: an engineering degree from one of the best, Georgia Tech. I made him proud, and that meant a lot to me. I always sought to bond with people more than the materials I chose to study. Again, feeling like a fraud.

I continued to lean on my father's mentorship; he was a hard-working IBM Dad, extremely loyal to their code of conduct, and a dedicated problem-solver. I had the analytical skills of an engineer but the passion of a justice warrior for doing what made sense and standing up for the people who maybe felt like I had - no real sense of belonging. Eventually, I became a young woman in the tech industry, pointing out how to improve things. I was direct in how I showed up in business, assuming results mattered most. I didn't know that seeing things clearly would be an affront to others.

I knew I could make a difference, so I felt compelled to act and often speak up. What I didn't expect was the backlash that I would face. Internal politics made no logical sense to me. Disconnects caused adversity throughout my life. In a world where we are all so different in sending, receiving, and processing information, we are bound to have a wide spectrum of preferences, styles, and speeds. I used to think, *"If I stay true to my heart, someday I'll be recognized for my intent and contribution."*

Life doesn't work out the way you expect it. My relationship with language and interpreting information became challenging as I navigated life. Just like with people. Sometimes, I allowed it to become a roadblock. Roadblocks: I'd visualize one every time that word got used.

"Can you remove roadblocks?" Hearing that question made me freeze.

My knee-jerk response was to think, *"No way! It's a gigantic cement barricade. Give me a problem, and I can solve it."* Also, I was thinking, *"What if **you** are the roadblock?"* I took on almost any challenge with perseverance. Most often, I sniffed out the deeper problems.

I started asking smart enough questions so that we would hit our goals. I strategized how to expose the root cause of real issues. It caused discomfort and alienated me, but my purpose remained steadfast, so I couldn't reconcile this. I felt so at odds with myself. Who I was did not feel embraced or celebrated. I thought that was wrong, and I couldn't stop myself.

I had many significant setbacks. I tried to learn, grow, and evolve, but ultimately, I knew I was stuck with who I was at the core. The problem was, I loved her. I still do. I am okay with her. It seemed like *everyone else* was not. No leader stood up to take me under their wing. I felt alone, abandoned, and abused.

So many people fall through the cracks. Those seen as strong are often treated like they don't need support. Our society can be performative; beyond tokenization, people often ostracize those who don't fit a certain mold. I've sat in that not-so-sweet spot my whole life. I thought, *"I will never fit in. I will never belong."* I felt abandoned by the people I was bringing in the results for. I was taught to keep learning and trying different things. So, I did. It still wasn't working.

As a project manager, I coach others to bring visions to reality. I had the urge to protect others from how I never felt protected except by my mom. She has people's backs. I was trying to do the same. When I had the foresight to see problems arise, I would speak up pre-emptively, *"Let me save you from this headache, time, or pain!".* My favorite gift is handing others my content and lessons packaged as if on a silver platter, so they don't have to suffer.

It frustrated me when I noticed that not everyone felt compelled to do the same. Everyone could use some help when they are in a mess. Everyone could use support. I recognized the need for people to nurture each other as part of the formula for success.

Remarkable things happen when you have intention, focus, discipline, and a responsible framework. It sounds so simple and obvious, but here's potentially a new angle. You must be willing to be unconventionally curious. In that way, you expand your ability to see previously hidden opportunities. When we're shut out, often, we also shut down.

Accept and love yourself because although it may feel scary and different, I'll tell you why it's the best ride ever. You'll feel like a jaguar cutting through the jungle to find prey. You'll discover a life of abundance by being the trailblazer you were meant to be. Although you may struggle, you'll realize you were meant for a different path.

Your new lens will be what makes you special. You offer a fresh perspective that nobody gets to take away from you. There's not one person, no automation, nothing that can take away the experiences that only you've lived, with the information you've processed, with your mind. You can tap into this if you haven't already begun.

When trying to reach big dreams, it usually requires a lot of support to make it happen. Think CEOs, entrepreneurs, community leaders, pretty much anyone! We need others to get stuff done. You are a pioneer in your journey. At the same time, it's possible to support others in theirs. We don't have to be Givers *or* Takers. We can create balance.

I also believe you won't accomplish much if your team looks, acts, and thinks exactly like you do. Creativity doesn't come from that. Do you seek innovation or validation?

When a diverse group is excited about a vision or goal, working under the same value system and honoring it, they are more likely to be creative and supportive, uplifting each other through collective inspiration. For example, this anthology is a team effort; we all created energy through it. We are already a success just for the experience. Beautiful bonds were built.

My strength in adversity comes from a childhood of being different and seeking others who could relate to that feeling. Through that, I developed a keen eye for seeking the unique value of each person. Imagine my surprise that others don't have that inclination, and we all continue to suffer because of it. It ignited me to coach others to discover and hone this skill.

If we all felt seen, valued, and accepted for exactly who we are, think about the possibilities that may have come to fruition. Human instinct is to do what keeps us safe. Blending in is often the default when you've been raised to value similarities. Many people still look to see what everyone else is doing first. I'm sure I do it too. Being part of a tribe makes us feel connected and protected. However, it can limit us if the tribe is not a system of true acceptance.

My ability to seek my tribe through curiosity and form a unique cast of characters has given me strength. My passion is to let others know it's okay to be the disruption they are or long

DR. CONSTANCE LEYLAND

to be. Through that, you may find you have many tribes to meet your different goals. We see this happening in business today. Project teams are like mini tribes. Please, just don't forget the law of reciprocity. It exists for a reason. We must take care of each other.

The most beautiful place is to wander naturally, like a child free to flow with imagination. You are free to roam when putting together the pieces of your life puzzle. Gathering your tribes! Don't allow anyone to make you feel stuck. I'll go to places where I can let people hang out with *their* fractions, hop right over those heavy cement barricades, and align my goals with those who want to thrive in the grey zone. When you set yourself free, you are.

The world is full of incredible people and opportunities! You are never stuck if you don't want to be. All you must do is use your mind to imagine the life you want, be curious enough to chase it down, and put the right people in your path. Together, you will be compelled to celebrate yourself, take steps forward, and no longer see your differences as adversity; rather as your superpower of healthy checks and balances, breaking up monotony, learning to empathize, and adapting. You'll change unproductive behaviors and supercharge the spirit of other trailblazers.

As a project manager, I've navigated through adversity by adhering to my purpose-driven path, which I crafted uniquely. It's been a journey of self-exploration like no other. Both personally and professionally, I am Kinga. I know who I am.

Ground yourself in who you are, stay curious and open-minded, open your heart, be kind, and demand no less from the people around you. Together, we can forge ahead, leveraging our collective strengths and experiences. It's in the power of community, seeking opportunities, and creating systems of acceptance that we can overcome any challenge and achieve anything.

I am the CEO & Founder of Execute Your Intentions, LLC. I aim to energize and equip leaders
to forge exceptional business outcomes through inclusive environments. Through dynamic online courses, interactive workshops, and agile program/project management content, I bring collective values and ambitions to life.

Formerly a VP of Project Management, I spent decades leading transformations in various growth stages, leadership models, mergers & acquisitions in the technology arena.

Follow me on LinkedIn https://www.linkedin.com/in/kingavajda/

https://executeyourintentions.com/

This chapter is dedicated to my parents; both of whom I honor and am amazed at what they have survived. They were and continue to be unwavering supporters in my life. I have a profound sense of standing up for what I believe in because of them. With that, may our legacy, our strength and core values live on.

The ADHD Advantage: Thriving in Life's Grey Zone

By: Dr. Constance Leyland

The Odyssey of Jipping: Navigating the Storms

In the shadowed lanes of a forgotten part of town, where echoes of the past mingled with whispers of the present, a young girl named Jipping forged her path through life. Marked by the scars of abandonment and the restless tide of ADHD, her journey was a testament to the resilience of the human spirit in the face of relentless adversity.

Jipping's life was a constellation of challenges, each star a story of struggle and perseverance. Her earliest memories were veiled in mystery, a void where the warmth of familial bonds should have been. This absence carved a deep longing in her heart, a yearning for a connection that seemed forever unfulfilled. Coupled with her ADHD, which painted her perceptions of the world in vibrant yet overwhelming strokes, Jipping found herself perpetually out of sync with her surroundings.

Though a crucible of creativity, the vibrant chaos of her mind often left her adrift in a sea of misunderstanding. In school, where conformity was the unspoken currency of acceptance, Jipping's differences became her albatross. Her thoughts raced ahead in classrooms, leaping from idea to idea while her peers moved in a lockstep that felt foreign to her. Her attempts to communicate her whirlwind of thoughts often tangled in her tongue, making her words misunderstood or mocked.

A specific incident etched itself into the fabric of her being, a moment that encapsulated her struggles and the cruelty of misunderstanding. During a science class, a project on the solar system became the battleground for her challenges. Tasked with creating a model, Jipping's mind envisioned a masterpiece, representing not just planets but the unseen forces that bound them. Her excitement was palpable, her ideas ambitious and far-reaching, fueled by the boundless energy of her ADHD.

But ambition, when coupled with ADHD, can be a double-edged sword. Her project sprawled out of control, and each attempt to harness her creativity led further away from completion. The deadline loomed like a storm cloud, and Jipping's model lay unfinished, a testament to her struggles with focus and organization.

The unveiling of the projects became a day of reckoning. As classmates presented their neatly finished models, Jipping's turn approached with the inevitability of a rising tide. Her explanation of the unfinished state of her model, filled with passion for the subject but lacking the expected results, became fodder for ridicule. Laughter filled the room, not at the ideas she cherished but at their incomplete realization. "Jipping's world," they jeered, a phrase that haunted her in the halls, a cruel nickname that underscored her sense of isolation and difference.

This moment of public humiliation was a microcosm of Jipping's daily battles. Bullied and ostracized for her differences, the scars of abandonment deepened, reinforcing her feelings of being an outsider in a world that valued conformity over creativity.

Yet, within this crucible of hardship, Jipping's true strength was forged. Her journey through bullying and misunderstanding taught her the profound resilience of the human spirit. She began to see her ADHD not as a flaw but as a fount of creativity, her capacity for divergent thinking a gift rather than a curse. She embraced her unique perspective on the world, finding solace and expression in art and poetry, where the vividness of her imagination could be celebrated without bounds.

In time, Jipping's narrative transformed from one of victimhood to victory. Her art became a bridge between her inner world and the outside, communicating the beauty she saw in the chaos. Through her poetry, she gave voice to the pain of abandonment and the strength found in solitude, her words resonating with others who felt misunderstood.

Jipping's odyssey from the shadows of bullying and abandonment to the light of self-acceptance and expression is a beacon to all who navigate the stormy seas of difference. Her story is a testament to the power of embracing one's uniqueness, proving that the darkest trials can lead to the most luminous discoveries of self. In the tapestry of human experience, Jipping's journey is a vibrant thread, weaving resilience, creativity, and hope into the fabric of life. In the complex mosaic of human neurodiversity, ADHD (Attention Deficit Hyperactivity Disorder) threads its way through the complex psychological elements of being neurodivergent. It often is misconstrued as a flaw rather than an asset. This chapter delves into the nuanced understanding of ADHD, illustrating how what once seemed insurmountable obstacles in my younger years have morphed into unparalleled strengths in the professional realm. Through a personal journey interwoven with the latest research, we explore why hiring individuals with ADHD can significantly benefit your company, transcending conventional perceptions and thriving in life's grey zone.

The Misunderstood Potential

Growing up with ADHD was akin to being a ship adrift in a vast ocean, where every wave of interest carried me further away from my intended destination. Projects started with enthusiasm and were left in the wake of new, more exciting pursuits, leading to a mosaic of unfinished tasks. With its rigid structure and demand for sustained attention, the conventional schooling system felt like a square peg in a round hole scenario for someone whose mind raced with the speed of a thousand horses. This inability to conform to traditional expectations often depicted underachievement and unreliability.

However, the very essence of ADHD that seemed to be a detriment in my formative years has blossomed into my greatest asset in the professional world. The ADHD brain is not deficient; it is merely different. It is a brain characterized by rapid-fire associative thinking, a constant search for stimulation, and an ability to make quantum leaps in creativity and problem-solving. These traits can be harnessed in the right environment to propel innovation and drive.

Harnessing the ADHD Advantage

Companies thriving in the modern economy recognize that innovation and agility are paramount to organizations' culture. The ADHD mind is tailor-made for such an environment. Here's why hiring someone with ADHD is not just an act of inclusivity but a strategic advantage:

Hyperfocus: Contrary to popular belief, individuals with ADHD can achieve a state of hyperfocus, diving deep into tasks that genuinely interest them. This intense concentration can lead to breakthroughs and innovations that might elude a neurotypical mind.

Creativity and Innovation: The ADHD brain thrives on novelty and complexity. It sees connections where others see disjointed data, leading to creative solutions and innovative ideas that can keep a company at the cutting edge of its industry.

Risk Tolerance: The inclination towards novelty and exploration makes individuals with ADHD more open to taking calculated risks, a necessary component of growth and innovation in business.

Resilience: Having navigated the challenges of growing up with ADHD, individuals develop unparalleled resilience and adaptability. This grit becomes a valuable asset in navigating the uncertainties of the business world.

From Liability to Asset: A Personal Transformation

My journey from being perceived as a liability to becoming an asset is a testament to the untapped potential of individuals with ADHD. Embracing my neurodiversity, I learned to channel the kaleidoscope of my thoughts into innovative projects and leadership roles. The key was finding an environment that valued diversity of thought and encouraged exploration. In such spaces, my propensity for boredom transformed into a quest for innovation, leading teams to explore uncharted territories and develop groundbreaking solutions.

This transition had its challenges. It required self-awareness, strategies to harness my strengths, and an environment accommodating different working styles. Yet, the journey underscored a critical insight: in the grey zone of life, where ambiguity and complexity reign, the ADHD mind is surviving and thriving.

Embracing Neurodiversity in the Workplace

The narrative of ADHD needs to shift from viewing it as a disorder to recognizing it as a different order of cognition that brings unique strengths to the table. Companies that are willing to step beyond traditional boundaries and leverage the ADHD advantage will find themselves enriched by a workforce that is resilient, innovative, and unafraid of challenges.

As we move forward, let us redefine what it means to be an asset to a company. In the grey zone of life and work, those with ADHD are not just fitting in; they are standing out, driving innovation, and redefining success. The future belongs to those who can think differently, and in the quest for innovation and resilience, the ADHD mind is a beacon of potential waiting to be unleashed.

Living with undiagnosed ADHD can feel like sailing a ship without a compass. For years, I navigated through life's waters, feeling perpetually out of sync with the world around me. My story isn't unique but deeply personal — a journey of self-discovery, understanding, and empowerment.

The Journey Begins

From early childhood, I felt the sting of difference. While others seemed to align effortlessly with the rhythms of daily life, I was the square peg in a round hole, constantly moving, thinking, and dreaming. The school was a challenge, though not for lack of intelligence. It was because my mind was a tempest of ideas that constantly shifted focus. I excelled in bursts of intense interest, only to struggle when the novelty wore off.

Friendships and relationships were equally complex. I was lively, enthusiastic, and intensely loyal, but the nuances of social interactions often eluded me. I missed cues, forgot important dates, and sometimes overwhelmed others with the intensity of my passions and pursuits.

Entering the workforce brought its own set of challenges. Traditional jobs felt like cages: constraining and suffocating. I thrived in environments that valued creativity and innovation yet struggled with organization, punctuality, and the monotony of routine tasks.

For years, I couldn't understand why I felt so different. It wasn't until adulthood, after a series of enlightening conversations and a deep dive into my behaviors and challenges, that I came to recognize the signs of ADHD in myself. This revelation was both shocking and liberating. Suddenly, the disparate pieces of my life's puzzle began to fit together.

Embracing ADHD: Strategies for Success

The journey of living with ADHD, diagnosed or not, is one of continuous learning and adaptation. Here are ten tips that ~~have~~ transformed my approach to work and life, leveraging my ADHD for productivity and success:

Understand Your ADHD: The first step to leveraging ADHD is understanding how it manifests in you. ADHD is a spectrum, and symptoms vary widely. Recognize your strengths and challenges, and use this knowledge to your advantage.

Structure and Routine: While routine might seem antithetical to the ADHD mind, establishing a flexible structure can provide the scaffolding needed for success. Start with simple routines for the beginning and end of your day.

Use Technology: Leverage technology to manage your tasks and time. Apps for time management, project management, and reminders can be incredibly helpful. Find tools that work for you and integrate them into your daily life.

Break Tasks Into Smaller Steps: Large projects can feel overwhelming. Break them down into smaller, manageable tasks, and focus on completing one step at a time.

Embrace the Power of Hyperfocus: Hyperfocus can be a superpower. Use it to your advantage by channeling it towards productive tasks and projects. Be mindful of what triggers your hyperfocus and use those triggers to get work done.

Set Clear Deadlines: The pressure of a deadline can be motivating. Set realistic deadlines for yourself, even small tasks, to provide a sense of urgency and purpose.

Exercise and Movement: Regular physical activity can significantly improve focus and mood. Incorporate exercise into your daily routine, even for a short walk or a quick workout.

Mindfulness and Meditation: Practices like mindfulness

and meditation can improve concentration, reduce impulsivity, and help manage stress. Even a few minutes a day can make a difference.

Seek Support: Whether it's from friends, family, or professionals, support is crucial. Consider joining an ADHD support group or working with a coach who specializes in ADHD.

Celebrate Your Wins: Recognize and celebrate your achievements, no matter how small. This reinforces positive behavior and boosts your confidence.

Leveraging ADHD in Project Management and Multitasking

In project management, juggling multiple tasks and ideas can be a strength. To leverage this in the context of ADHD, prioritize tasks based on urgency and importance. Use visual aids like charts and boards to keep track of progress and changes.

Effective multitasking requires understanding how to switch between tasks without losing focus or productivity. One strategy is to dedicate specific time to different tasks, using a timer to limit how long you spend on each before taking a short break or switching tasks.

A Personal Tale of Transformation

My journey of living unknowingly with ADHD has been a path of peaks and valleys. Learning to navigate my ADHD without prior knowledge was challenging, but it also taught me resilience, creativity, and the value of embracing my unique perspective. I've come to see my ADHD not as a hindrance but as a different way of interacting with the world—one that is full of potential and possibilities.

As I've implemented strategies for managing my ADHD, I've noticed a profound shift in my productivity and overall satisfaction. Tasks that once seemed daunting are now manageable. I've learned to channel my hyperfocus for success, turning my passion into my profession. My relationships have deepened, and I've found communities that understand and celebrate the unique contributions of individuals with ADHD.

Living with undiagnosed ADHD is like navigating a complex labyrinth filled with unexpected turns and hidden treasures. It's a journey of constant discovery, requiring patience, understanding, and a willingness to adapt. By embracing my ADHD and leveraging it through effective strategies, I've transformed my challenges into assets. My life is a testament to the fact that, with the right approach, individuals with ADHD can manage and thrive, turning their vibrant chaos into a symphony of success.

Living with adult ADHD can often feel like walking a tightrope, constantly seeking a balance between the bustling energy of your mind and the demands of daily life. However, finding harmony and happiness at work and in your personal life is not only possible, it's within your reach. Here are some strategies to help you navigate this journey.

Embrace Self-Awareness

The foundation of finding balance with adult ADHD starts with self-awareness. Understand how ADHD affects you —your strengths, challenges, and triggers. This self-knowledge is crucial for developing coping strategies that work for you. Recognizing your unique patterns of behavior and thought can help you anticipate and mitigate challenges before they arise.

Create Structured Routines

While spontaneity can be exhilarating, structure is your ally. Develop routines that provide a predictable framework for your day. This doesn't mean stifling your spontaneity but rather creating a stable base from which to explore. Simple routines, like morning preparations or evening wind-down activities, can significantly reduce decision fatigue and make daily tasks more manageable.

Prioritize and Organize

With many ideas and tasks vying for your attention, it's essential to prioritize. Use tools and methods that resonate with you, like lists, apps, or visual boards, to organize your responsibilities. Focus on what needs immediate attention and what can wait. This approach can help reduce feeling overwhelmed and increase your sense of control and accomplishment.

Harness Your Hyperfocus

Hyperfocus can be a double-edged sword, leading you to lose track of time on interests while neglecting other essential tasks. Learn to recognize the signs of hyperfocus and gently guide it toward productive activities. Set alarms or reminders to take breaks or shift to other tasks, ensuring a more balanced distribution of your time and energy.

Set Boundaries

Setting clear boundaries is crucial for maintaining balance. This includes work-life boundaries, such as specific work hours and personal time, and emotional boundaries, including knowing when to say no. Protecting your time and energy allows you to be more present and effective in both work and personal endeavors.

Embrace Flexibility

While structure is important, so is flexibility. ADHD can make some days more challenging than others. Be kind to yourself and adjust your expectations based on your feelings. Flexibility also means being open to trying new strategies or adjusting existing ones as your needs and circumstances change.

Seek Support

You don't have to navigate ADHD alone. Seek support from friends, family, or professionals who understand ADHD. Support groups, either in-person or online, can provide valuable insights and encouragement from others on a similar journey.

Cultivate Mindfulness

Mindfulness practices can improve focus, reduce impulsivity, and help manage stress. Techniques like meditation, deep breathing, or yoga can enhance one's awareness of the present moment, allowing one to engage more fully with one's work and personal life.

Pursue Passion Projects

Engaging in activities that spark joy and passion can provide a vital outlet for your energy and creativity. Whether it's a hobby, side project, or volunteer work, make time for pursuits that fulfill you beyond your professional achievements.

Celebrate Your Wins

Take time to acknowledge and celebrate your successes, no matter how small. Recognizing achievements can boost confidence and motivation, reinforcing positive patterns and behaviors.

Finding balance with adult ADHD is a dynamic process that requires patience, self-compassion, and persistence. By embracing your unique way of experiencing the world, you can create a fulfilling life that honors your challenges and extraordinary strengths. Remember, ADHD does not define you —it's just one part of the complex, vibrant person you are. Remember that you are terrific with unique abilities and qualities. Finding who you are and where you blossom is part of a journey one has to embark on. Remember to be kind to yourself.

Dr. Leyland is a distinguished academic and professional with a rich educational background in Communication, Organizational Leadership, Cybersecurity, and International Business. Their career spans roles as a Professor, Dean, TV, and Podcast Host, and three times International Best-Selling co-author, blending academic knowledge with real-world application. Dr. Leyland excels in business education, employing engaging teaching methods to inspire students. Their leadership as a Dean has fostered academic excellence and a supportive learning environment, enhancing faculty and student diversity. Dr. Leyland's venture into podcasting offers a platform for intellectual dialogue, while their publications contribute significantly to academia. They are pursuing further studies in I/O Psychology, demonstrating an unwavering commitment to understanding organizational and human behavior dynamics. Dr. Leyland's continuous pursuit of knowledge and its impact on academia and media underscore their role as pivotal in both fields, continually pushing the boundaries of intellectual and professional advancement.

To my support system, my husband, Tom Leyland, and my kids, Angelina Leyland and Annabella Leyland. Mommy loves you to the moon and back, and I would gladly take all your pain for your happiness. May you find happiness in your life.

Made in the USA
Columbia, SC
05 April 2024

34020954R00161